WHAT KANSAS CITIANS ARE SAYING ABOUT THIS PUBLICATION...

*"**Surviving Divorce in Kansas City** is a great tool and resource for anyone experiencing divorce. Because the information is concise and easy to follow, this book is a good place to start the search for guidance not only about how to survive your divorce but also how you start on your new life."*

— Carol Roeder-Esser, L.S.C.S.W.
Johnson County Mental Health Center

■ ■ ■ ■

*"**Surviving Divorce in Kansas City** is an excellent 'tool of the trade' for anyone involved in the practice of family law. Linda Sanchez has answered the commonly asked questions about all aspects of the divorce process and opened the door for many referral opportunities. I have received several telephone inquiries as a result of being listed in this publication."*

— Donna M. Manning
Manning & Smith
Attorneys at Law

■ ■ ■ ■

"The book was quite helpful in the early stages of the divorce and continues to be an excellent resource. It provided some words of comfort and direction, as well as a much needed source of information about where to get additional help. Since then, I have referred to it several times to revisit some of the topics discussed as well as to find other resources that may be of benefit as the divorce proceeding continues."

— William E. Ekey
Kansas City, Missouri

To my inspiration and strength –
Andrew Henry Mulligan

By Linda Sanchez

Disclaimer: This book is designed to provide accurate information in regard to the subject matter covered. It is sold with the understanding that the publisher is not engaged in rendering legal, accounting, psychological, medical or professional service. Authors do not intend to render forgoing services by providing the text which is attributed to them. If legal advice or other expert assistance is required, the services of a competent professional person should be sought.

The authors and publisher are not responsible to any person or organization for any loss directly or indirectly caused by information contained in this book.

The text (excluding the advertisements) represents the opinions of the authors listed. Each section that is attributed to a particular author represents the opinion of that author alone and is not necessarily the opinion of the author of another section.

This book contains advertisements and listings paid for by individuals and organizations that provide products and services in the Kansas City metropolitan area relating to divorce. While the author and publisher have made a reasonable effort to ensure that the text of this book (other than the advertisements) are accurate; they have not been able to verify the accuracy of the advertisements.

Copyright 1999 by Linda Sanchez. All rights reserved. Printed in the United States of America.
Second printing, revised.

No part of this publication may be reproduced, stored in a retrieval system, or transmitted in any form by any means, electronic, mechanical photocopying, recording or otherwise without the prior written permission of the publisher.

Library of Congress Catalog Card Number 98-90849

ISBN# 0-9656174-1-6

As You Like It
by Simone
Fine Designs for You

Jewelry Manufacturing

4801 Jefferson • Kansas City, Mo 64112
on the Country Club Plaza

816-531-5591 • 1-800-229-8462

About the Author

LINDA SANCHEZ received her Bachelor's degree in Journalism and Mass Communications and Modern Languages from Kansas State University and has eleven years' experience in marketing and promotion. Her background combined with her personal experience with the divorce process in Kansas City led to the creation of *Surviving Divorce in Kansas City.* Linda experienced pain and frustration during her divorce because she was unaware of area resources. This led to her determination to help others by providing them with the information they need to survive divorce and eventually thrive in their new life.

Linda Sanchez

■

Acknowledgments

Advisory Board

Betty Dawson, R.N./Women's Health Educator
The University of Kansas Medical Center

Kent Hermes/Writer/Producer
Corporate Video

Tajquah Hudson
Business Development Officer
The University of Kansas Medical Center

Robert Unell/Owner
Unell Associates/Publisher *Twins Magazine*

Jean Humphrey/Director
Johnson County Family Life

Tom Mulligan/Consultant
Thomas Performance Group

Nicole Sanchez/Retired Teacher
Unified School District 475

Carla Shelton Everhart/President
United Way of Wyandotte County

Michael J. Albano/Attorney
Welch, Martin, Albano & Manners, P.C.

Barbara C. Thompson, Ph.D./Psychologist
Professional Psychological Institute

Katherine White, M.S./Psychologist
Professional Psychological Institute

∎

Book Design: Cole Design & Production, Rosemary Holderby

Cover Illustration: Tom McFarland

A Letter From a Survivor

Dear Friend:

After the first edition of *Surviving Divorce in Kansas City* became available, I heard from many Kansas Citians who were going through or who had just gone through a divorce. I was also contacted by individuals who work in the divorce service industry such as attorneys and counselors. Everyone encouraged me to continue with this publication that has, in the last year, been helpful to so many people living in Kansas City.

It is because of the gratitude I received, as well as the encouragement from the business community, that this second edition is now available. The editorial wisdom provided from the contributing writers remains the one constant from the last edition. This new edition also includes expanded and updated listings in the resource sections after each chapter.

In updating the resource sections, I again have discovered individuals in Kansas City who are quality professionals with the best interests of their clients at heart. You will notice that some have even provided display messages about their product or service in order to present you with more details about what they can do for you. Information on new opportunities for counseling, education and training, as well as participating in social activities, is also included in this edition.

It has been four years since my divorce and I continue to have a satisfying and challenging new life. However, because of the life lessons learned in divorce and other painful transitions, I know that strength in family, friends and more importantly, in myself, will guide me through whatever happens next. It is my hope that *Surviving Divorce in Kansas City* continues to provide strength through emotional support and practical wisdom to those who are experiencing this very difficult time.

Best regards,

Linda Sanchez

Linda Sanchez

TABLE OF CONTENTS

Introduction
- The How and Why of Using This Book 9
- You're Not Just a Statistic But Here They Are Anyway 10

Meeting Your Emotional Needs *11*
- Taking Care of Your Spiritual and Physical Health 12
- Overwhelming Feelings of Sadness, Guilt, Anger and Hurt: How, Where, What and When to Seek Counseling 14
- How Friends and Family Can Help 17
- Getting Through the Workday (Dos and Don'ts on the Job) 19
- Reading, Music, Volunteering and Hot Baths (All of These Really Do Help) 20
- Resource Listing 32

Parenting Before, During and After Divorce *23*
- Children and Divorce 24
- Divorced Dads: Their Essential Influence 27
- What to Look for in the Child Care Industry 30
- Resource Listing 32

What to Expect From the Legal Side *37*
- The Divorce Proceedings 38
- Finding a Lawyer in Kansas City 40
- The Importance of Communication 43
- Attorney's Fees and Costs 45
- Divorce in Missouri and Kansas: Differences and Similarities 47
- Resource Listing 52

7

TABLE OF CONTENTS

Financial Decisions: Making the Right Choices ... 57
How to Navigate Through Divorce
and Build Financial Security 58
Finding/Selling Your Home in Kansas City 62
Resource Listing 64

Recovery and Planning for a New Life 67
Connecting with Self Before Reconnecting 68
Divorce and Vocational Concerns 71
Taking Advantage of the Educational
Opportunities in Kansas City 74
Health and Beauty: Now's the Time to Indulge 75
Your Time Has Come to See the World:
Traveling to and From Kansas City 77
Saving Valuable Time:
Housing/Lawn/Pet Care Services 78
Resource Listing 79

Index of Resource Listings 83

The How and Why of Using This Book

Getting married, having children, moving to a new town – all of these are major transitions in life, and chances are you can easily get your hands on numerous publications that will take you step-by-step throughout each process. Why isn't divorce addressed in this same step-by-step manner? Divorce is truly a major transition in life that has been neglected by the directory publishing industry – until now.

At the time of divorce, people frequently make other transitions, like moving or returning to school. They need all the products and services that go along with these transitions such as housing, furnishings and career counseling. They also need help and support negotiating the legal system, coping with their divorces and developing new social lives. Going through the divorce process for the first time is overwhelming – top that with being in a highly emotional and stressed state of mind – this makes it ten times more difficult.

In doing research for this publication, I met many individuals in Kansas City who are quality professionals with the best interests of their clients at heart. Fortunately, most were able to become contributors to this publication and I am now able to bring to you all of the resources I wish would have been available to me at the time of my divorce.

Each section provides a 2-3 page overview of recommendations from area authors on the various topics prominent in a divorce situation – emotional needs, legal matters, finances, parenting and recovery. These overviews are not meant to provide in-depth information on each topic but rather to highlight important areas and point you in the direction of obtaining more information if you choose. After each editorial you will find a listing of various resources – names, addresses and telephone numbers in Kansas City for each topic.

There are hundreds of self-help publications that cover topics ranging from the emotional well-being of the individual, to parenting, and to the practical aspects of finances and law. However, there are no resources available that provide an individual with a step-by-step guide of local resources. *Surviving Divorce in Kansas City* is the resource to help you, your friend or family member experiencing divorce in Kansas City, navigate the process successfully.

■

You're Not Just a Statistic But Here They Are Anyway...

As you experience divorce, you may feel more alone than ever before...how could anyone be feeling the same way or having the same experiences as you? And to some extent you are right: no one *does* feel the same as you. However, the statistics reinforce the fact that you are not alone in experiencing divorce. The following chart provides an overview of divorce/annulments for the Kansas City area (defined by the ten counties listed).

The support of individuals experiencing similar situations can be very helpful. Support groups are available through counseling and social services as well as various religious organizations in the Kansas City area. See the resource directory on page 32 of this publication for more information.

KANSAS 1996 Statistics		MISSOURI 1995 Statistics	
Marriages	Divorces	Marriages	Divorces
20,657	10,779	44,900	26,800

Source: *Statistical Abstract of the United States, U.S. Department of Commerce, Economics and Statistics Administration, Bureau of Census.*

KANSAS CITY IN KANSAS – FOUR-COUNTY AREA 1996 Statistics		
County	Marriages	Divorces/Annulments
Johnson	2,678	777
Leavenworth	495	183
Miami	192	69
Wyandotte	1,307	565

Source: *Kansas Statistical Abstract 1997 Institute for Public Policy and Business Research, University of Kansas.*

KANSAS CITY IN MISSOURI – SIX-COUNTY AREA 1995 Statistics		
County	Marriages	Divorces/Annulments
Cass	582	415
Clay	1,481	881
Clinton	114	105
Jackson	5,862	2,705
Platte	485	384
Ray	137	115

Source: *Missouri Vital Statistics, 1995, Missouri Department of Health, Center for Health Information Management and Epidemiology.*

Meeting Your Emotional Needs

Taking Care of Your Spiritual and Physical Health 12

*Overwhelming Feelings of Sadness, Guilt,
Anger and Hurt; How, Where, What and
When to Seek Counseling* 14

How Friends and Family Can Help 17

*Getting Through the Workday
(Dos and Don'ts on the Job)* 19

*Reading, Music, Volunteering and Hot Baths
(All of These Really Do Help)* 20

Resource Listing 32

Contributing Writers

TOM JACOBS is a recording artist of reflective music, a teacher of yoga and a facilitator of workshops on the prayer of meditation. Tom is also a former Benedictine monk with degrees in Theology, Philosophy, Education and Music.

KATHERINE R. WHITE is a licensed psychologist maintaining two practice locations in the Greater Kansas City area. She works with individuals and families in a variety of areas including substance abuse, mood disorders, personality disorders, family and couples counseling and adjustment/crisis intervention. Katherine also has served as a consultant to various local and national entities providing critical incident stress debriefing, crisis intervention and comprehensive training. Her memberships include the American Psychology Association, the Missouri Psychology Association and the Greater Kansas City Psychological Association. Katherine, previously divorced, is happily remarried and the mother of three teenage daughters.

SURVIVING DIVORCE

Taking Care of Your Spiritual and Physical Health

by Tom Jacobs

As you read this article, you're probably in the midst of the swimming lesson of your life! Pain and loss teach us to swim in the Seas of Life as intensely as any teacher I've ever known. You're probably swallowing some unwanted salt water too, as you learn to swim the deep waters.

Tom Jacobs

Though none of us go out searching for ways to suffer, our greatest teacher, LIFE, is always around the corner encouraging us to stretch, evolve, change and grow. It's an invitation that either gently whispers in your ear or it screams to you in a megaphone!

Any time this invitation comes, it's a wake-up call to move forward with your life. And I'm sure you're aware of how much it actually wakes you up and gets your attention. And that's exactly what pain and/or loss is designed to do – wake us and get our attention!

Responding to the invitation demands our attention and our willingness to swim in the midst of rough waters. Fortunately, our inner spirit has no trouble swimming, but our emotional nature is sometimes reluctant to get in the water. I assure you that NOW is the best time ever to have hope. Even if your logical mind tells you otherwise, believe me, now is the best time to hold on to hope.

Hope is really another name for God. Since Hope/God is our origin, it's good to come home to the Source that guides and sustains us...even if the path is often as unclear as driving in fog. Despite the fog, there are people who know how to drive in the fog of unknowing; people who have sustained the worst of conditions.

Oftentimes the sting of pain and loss compels us to deepen our union with God. This deepening can be done in many ways including:

- learning meditation
- taking walks
- reading
- taking an exercise class
- practicing yoga and/or tai chi
- jogging
- enjoying a warm bath
- watching a good movie
- spending time with a friend
- having some involvement in a volunteer service
- getting involved with your church or synagogue

EMOTIONAL

Time alone is also very healthy, especially if it's wisely balanced with spending time with people.

It's good to remember that our spiritual path is not just something from the neck up, but also involves the entire body. Your body is the temple of God and is truly enlivened with energy and new life as you move and stretch and involve yourself in cardiovascular activities. Part of the secret is to BALANCE your active life with your times of introspection and relaxation.

Life is essentially waking you up to realize (once again) that you have options and new opportunities with which to paint a new picture on the canvas of your life. Some of the practices mentioned above are wonderful ways to enable yourself to paint a new picture on your canvas and deepen your union with God all in one experience. Take advantage of this transformative time and remember that the Maker of the Ear is not deaf.

SURVIVING DIVORCE

Overwhelming Feelings of Sadness, Guilt, Anger and Hurt; How, Where, What and When to Seek Counseling

by Katherine R. White, M.S.

Divorce is difficult for all parties involved, no matter what the circumstances. If the person we selected to marry no longer fulfills that role, it is a loss – a loss of our future as we had once pictured it.

Loss brings forth all sorts of emotions and responses including anger, sadness, guilt, hurt, denial and withdrawal. The responses are different for everyone, but everyone processes grief *in some way*. Those persons emotionally close to us, our family and friends, often wish to help. They offer this help in many ways. They may offer advice, telling us what we should or could do, or they may regress into their own experience and process their own unattended grief. Sometimes they will be more patient and listen, giving us the ear we so desperately need just to be heard. However, with all this, they may not have the wisdom to say what we need to hear; they may be either fearful of making a mistake or unsure of what direct support to offer. It is most helpful if we can find a neutral support person or group to assist in working through the loss. This need for support is the primary reason persons going through the trauma of divorce seek support from a mental health professional. (Seeking support from a *mental health professional* does not mean there is something wrong with your mental health. It is simply a term to differentiate this professional from others. Therefore, from here on I will refer to the mental health professional simply as the *professional.*)

Below are answers to some of the questions you may ask yourself with regard to professional support as you go through this challenging experience in your life.

How do I know I need professional support?

Everyone could benefit from some type of professional support; after all, two heads are always better than one, especially if one of the heads has been trained to look at the issues and can assist in supporting your needs more effectively. However, not everyone necessarily *needs* professional support. The keys to seeking professional support are:

1) do I exhibit symptoms which would place me at risk for physical illness due to this stress? i.e., difficulty sleeping, change in eating habits, depressed/agitated mood, difficulty concentrating, frequent crying spells/anger outbursts, feelings of confusion, apathy, sadness or irritability much of the time, and/or

2) do I feel better when I have someone to talk to who can be neutral with me and help me sort through the confusion, anger, etc.

If you answer yes to either one or both of these questions, it may be in your best interest to seek the support of a mental health professional. This will give you a sounding board to sort through the grief and loss issues and assist you in feeling better faster. It will not take away the hurt, only assist in building the hope.

Where do I go to get this professional support?

First of all, see what resources exist within your personal/professional network. Oftentimes your employer or the employer of your spouse will offer an Employee Assistance Program. This program is designed to review your needs and either offer short-term support directly or make appropriate referral based on your need, location, insurance, etc. If this service is not available, review what insurance benefits are available and how to access those for yourself. It is important to review the policy for all HMO/PPO, Managed Care limitations. If you are unsure, contact the Personnel Department of the company through which the insurance is purchased. In the case of the spouse's benefits being available, most policies provide coverage until the divorce is final, and even then you have the option to continue with the service for a fee. If no benefits exist to assist you, contact area social service agencies such as Heart of America Family Services or Catholic Charities. Their phone numbers and addresses can be found on page 32 of this book.

What are the key factors to selecting the appropriate mental health professional?

Research has found that the primary factors leading to success in therapy are a combination of the *relationship* between the individual and the professional, and the *motivation* of the individual. It is not as important what kind of therapist or counselor you see; the important piece is that the individual works for *you*. Decide what factors are important to you, i.e., gender, age, location, philosophy, previous experience, etc. And don't be shy about these needs. You may want to interview a potential provider before entering into a therapeutic relationship. This is totally acceptable in the profession. Part of getting through the loss is learning ways to take care of yourself. Be assertive. Advise the potential providers that you are "interviewing potential providers." They should be willing to work with you, offering information with regard to themselves and a short appointment to review the potential for working together. If they are unwilling to do this, move on. You don't buy a car before you drive it; don't select a therapist without assessing the fit.

When do I know I've completed the process?

This is a difficult thing to assess, because the therapeutic relationship is very supportive and begins to feel very safe and nurturing. However, a good professional will work with you to work *out* of therapy, usually anywhere from six months to two years. The grieving process does tend to maintain a twelve-month cycle and we usually begin to see significant healing within that timeframe. Again, everyone is different. Don't judge your progress by someone else. Be patient with yourself. It takes time. I offer a quote which has meant so much to me through my lifetime, including the time of my divorce. "Listening to your heart, finding out who you are, is not simple. It takes time for the chatter to quiet down. In the silence of 'not doing' we begin to know what we feel. If we listen and hear what is being offered, then anything in life can be our guide. Listen." More than anything, painful experiences in life help us to know ourselves better. It does indeed take effort to hear ourselves and be patient. Don't rush. You will get there. Trust yourself.

EMOTIONAL

How Friends and Family Can Help

by Katherine R. White, M.S.

In divorce, our family and friends are usually the primary support in the healing process. Their listening ears and words of encouragement are essential in our recovery. Most of the time they are very eager and willing to help. However, they may not know the best way to do so. Below are some simple tips for family and friends to assist them in supporting your grief and loss effectively. This section is written primarily to them.

Here are some dos and don'ts for you as a family/friend of someone going through divorce. These suggestions are not intended to be all-inclusive regarding your loved one's need for support. It is a beginning place and guidelines for more effective support.

- **Don't judge the decision they have made to divorce.** Divorce is very difficult and often a decision that is made after much thought and emotional turmoil. It may not be the choice you would make for them but remember, everyone does life differently. Give them the chance to work through this themselves.

- **Don't give unsolicited advice.** Most individuals know from their own understanding of life what they can and should do. This decision-making process may take time and the clarity may not be immediate, but most of the time the answers will come. Be patient. Your reality is not the same as the person in the situation and your answers will not necessarily be their answers.

- **Don't reject or abandon your loved one.** The times we need support most are often the times we ask for it the least. This means that you, the family and friends, will need to be proactive in your giving of support. Little things like cards and letters, spontaneous phone calls, invitations for "fun," as well as simply listening over coffee will mean so much, especially when they are feeling so alone. Their loss is real. Don't leave them now. They truly cannot help where they are.

- **Don't be too overbearing with your "support."** Intermittent support as noted above is wonderful. *Constant* attention may give the message that they cannot take care of themselves. Don't suffocate them. Listen to what they are saying about what they need, feel, think, etc., and respond to them. If you are unclear, ask. Asking shows you truly care and offers the individual a direct way to get his/her needs met. If they are unsure of what they need, trust your instincts and proceed cautiously. If you err, do it on the side of genuine support, which is very different from control.

SURVIVING DIVORCE

- **Don't expect too much.** Divorcing individuals go through several emotional stages. Try not to expect and anticipate what they will do or how they *should* respond. And most of all, let them be where they are. It may be difficult to watch loved ones in this place in life without wanting to move them out of it. After all, when they hurt, you hurt. You may have temporarily lost your companion or playmate and you may be experiencing your own loss. Be patient. They will get better and life will return to some sense of normalcy.

- **Do provide a safe place.** Just being there, and being constant can be the best gift you can give. Grief and loss create great needs, often unpredictable ones. Just "be there." It is the greatest source of hope they can have.

- **Do encourage and offer insight.** We have all experienced loss in life. You are no exception. In loss, it is always comforting to know that others have felt, responded, thought, in a similar way. It takes away the feeling of isolation they will feel in these lonely times.

- **Do seek support for yourself.** When someone we love is hurting, we hurt. We cannot be of support to them if we don't get the support we need as well. You may need to expand your support network or seek counseling for yourself. Be proactive. It may set an example for them to do the same.

EMOTIONAL

Getting Through the Workday
(Dos and Don'ts on the Job)   by Kathrine R. White, M.S.

When we divorce, it can feel at times like our world is falling apart. Unfortunately, others don't appreciate or understand our "out of control" feelings. We are expected to still maintain our daily routine, despite the hurt and confusion. A part of this daily routine is going to work. How we cope at work can be essential in how we get through the divorce process intact. Below are some tips on how to handle the workplace most effectively.

- **Advise your superiors** of what you are going through in order for them to understand the possible changes in your behavior. Do this in a brief fashion, offering only the facts that are pertinent to your work situation. Examples may be changes in child care schedules; additional phone calls from attorneys, daycare, etc.; additional time off for appointments, etc.

- **Don't expect special consideration** from fellow employees or supervisors. This is your personal life and expecting that the workplace will offer special considerations may only serve to disappoint and discourage you further.

- **Be selective in whom you confide your personal issues.** Oftentimes we trust others too much, especially when we are vulnerable. The information you offer may be misconstrued or taken negatively, only to be used against you in the future.

- **Be aware of how others perceive you** as you go through the divorce process. People still place a negative stigma on divorce and may treat you differently, just because you are no longer a part of a "couple." Make every effort to establish your identity and encourage others to see you as a capable individual. Include yourself in work activities as an individual when you can and establish with your co-workers that this is an acceptable place for them to see you as well.

- **Be aware** of the discomfort others may have in your presence. Discussions with regard to upcoming marriage or childbirth may be awkward. Address these issues directly, offering brief explanations for what your comfort zones are; this allows for more open communication. If you sense resistance or withdrawal from others, it is appropriate to gently confront them to establish what you need to get through this time.

- **Do not be afraid** to take time off when you need it. Depression and sadness are a part of the grief process and can be overwhelming, debilitating at times. Be aware of your limits and take the time you need to heal yourself. Your mental health is as important as your physical health and, in fact, the two cannot be separated. If you are mentally drained, your physical self will respond in kind.

SURVIVING DIVORCE

Reading, Music, Volunteering and Hot Baths
(All of These Really Do Help)
by Linda Sanchez

You may already designate time in your life for reading, music, volunteering and hot baths. If so, you are probably very familiar with how these activities contribute to personal comfort and satisfaction.

Some of you, however, may not take the time to participate in any of these activities or perhaps your former spouse did not have an interest and therefore you never pursued them. Whatever the case, your opportunity is now here to explore one or all of these options: listening to your favorite song; volunteering at a hospital or museum; going to a concert or the theater; or reading a book during a good soak in the tub. These are all examples of activities that can help you get through this troubled time.

Kansas City residents are a very diverse group and therefore no list of recommended reading, entertainment and volunteer opportunities would sufficiently address the wide range of individual preferences. The following is only a sample of the many resources available in Kansas City.

Arts and Culture
Concert Line and Ticket Information 816/931-3330

Jazz Hot Line 816/763-1052

What's going on in K.C.? Look on-line: http://www.kansas city.com

Coffeehouses
Broadway Cafe 816/531-2432

East 51st Street Coffee House 816/756-3121

Java Cup Coffee House 913/385-5282

Westport Coffee House 816/756-3222

Dance
City in Motion Dance Theater 816/472-7828

Kansas City Friends of Alvin Ailey 816/471-6003

State Ballet of Missouri 816/931-2232

Westport Ballet 816/531-4330

Galleries
Byron Cohen/Lennie Berkowitz Gallery for Contemporary Art 816/421-5665

Central Park Gallery 816/471-7711

Dolphin Gallery 816/842-4415

Eth'nic Art 816/561-7600

Gallery North 816/421-4848

Grand Arts 816/421-6887

EMOTIONAL

Jan Weiner Gallery 816/931-8755

The Jayne Gallery 816/561-5333

Joan Cawley Gallery 913/599-2442

Leedy-Voulkos Art Center Gallery 816/474-1919

Museums
Agricultural Hall of Fame 913/721-1075

American Royal Museum 816/221-9800

Arabia Steamboat Museum 816/471-4030

Kansas City Museum 816/483-8300

Kemper Museum of Contemporary Art & Design 816/561-3737

Negro Leagues Baseball Museum 913/221-1920

Nelson-Atkins Museum of Art 816/561-4000

Music Organizations
Friends of Chamber Music 816/561-9999

Kansas City Chorale 816/931-7669

Kansas City Symphony Orchestra 816/471-0400

Lyric Opera 816/471-7344

Mutual Musicians Foundation 816/471-5212

Night Life – Blues
B.B.'s Lawnside Bar-B-Q 816/822-7427

Grand Emporium 816/531-1504

Harling's Upstairs 816/531-0303

The Roxy 913/236-6211

Night Life – Country
The Beaumont Club 816/561-2668

Guitars & Cadillacs 816/829-8200

Night Life – Jazz
Club 427 816/421-2582

The Club at Plaza III 816/753-0000

Club Mardi Gras 816/842-8463

Jardine's Restaurant & Jazz 816/561-6480

Jazz-A Louisiana Kitchen 816/531-5556

Phoenix Piano Bar & Grill 816/472-0001

Night Life – Rock
Atlantis and The Cave 816/753-0112

Blayney's 816/561-3747

Davey's Uptown 816/753-1909

The Hurricane 816/753-0884

The Levee 816/561-2821

Niener's 816/461-6955

Recommended Reading
See page 34

Theater
American Heartland Theatre 816/842-9999

Folly Theatre 816/474-4444

Midland Theatre 816/471-8600

Missouri Repertory Theatre 816/235-2700

Music Hall 816/274-2900

New Theatre Restaurant 913/649-7469

Quality Hill Playhouse 816/474-7529

Starlight Theatre 816/363-7827

Theatre for Young America 913/831-1400

Unicorn Theater 816/531-7529

Volunteer Opportunities*

Volunteer Center – Heart of America United Way
816/474-5112

Volunteer Center of the United Way of Wyandotte County 913/371-3674

Volunteer Center of Jackson County
816/252-2636

Volunteer Center of Johnson County
913/341-1792

The Volunteer Connection
816/472-4865

Humane Society of Greater Kansas City
913/371-3869

Wayside Waifs 816/761-8151

* Check with your local hospital, school or religious organization for volunteer opportunities also.

Parenting Before, During and After Divorce

Children and Divorce 24

Divorced Dads: Their Essential Influence 27

What to Look for in the Child Care Industry 30

Resource Listing 32

Contributing Writers

BARBARA C. THOMPSON is a managing partner for the Professional Psychological Institute in Kansas City, Missouri. Dr. Thompson has a Ph.D. in Counseling from the University of Missouri-Kansas City. Since 1977, Dr. Thompson has been providing psychological services in individual, marital, family, and group therapy. Dr. Thompson also has provided counseling services through the Jackson County Juvenile Court system and the Raytown School District. Her professional memberships include American Psychological Association; American Association of Counseling and Development; Missouri Psychological Association; and the Greater Kansas City Psychological Association.

TOM SCOTT is a psychotherapist/educational consultant with Responsive Centers for Psychology and Learning. Tom has facilitated numerous groups and workshops on Healing, Finding a Balance and Essential Parenting. Tom, a divorced dad and father of three, has recently organized an education and support group for men and their children who are in various stages of divorce. "Kansas City Center for Divorced Dads" provides a full range of emotional, mental and educational support services for divorced dads.

KAREN CLAYTON, The Child Care Association of Johnson County (CCAJC), a licensed Resource and Referral agency, has been providing child care referrals to parents who live and/or work in Johnson County since May of 1980. The Association also provides services, such as workshops, a resource library, curriculum materials, technical assistance, and the Child and Adult Care Food Program (for family child care providers) to early childhood professionals in Johnson County and throughout the Kansas City area. Karen Clayton joined the staff of CCAJC in 1987, and has been the executive director since 1992.

SURVIVING DIVORCE

Children and Divorce

by Barbara C. Thompson, Ph.D.

Divorce is a reality that directly or indirectly affects most people. "One out of two new marriages in the United States will eventually end in divorce, most of them within the first ten years… Because this high rate of divorce is expected to continue, over one-third of children today will experience a parental divorce" (Helping Children Cope with Divorce, *see page 35).*

Researchers who study divorce and its effects on children have indicated a need to distinguish between immediate, or short-term, reactions and long-term reactions (more than two years). Children's long-term reactions vary a great deal depending primarily on how the parents respond to the child during and after the divorce. Other factors that influence the reaction of a child will be the child's sex and age.

"The amount of parental harmony or disharmony children experience after divorce will be the most important determinant of their long-term adjustment" (*Helping Children Cope with Divorce,* see page 35).

The short-term reactions tend to be more consistent. Being aware of what you might expect from your children can help you to be alert to "red flags" that signal distress.

> **LEGAL TIP:**
> Contempt of court for failure to make court-ordered support payments or failure to permit court-ordered visitation may result in a jail sentence.
> ■

Informing the Children

Once the decision is made to divorce, both parents need to tell the children together. Decide with your spouse the best way to inform your children. It is crucial for parents to explain clearly that their decision to divorce is unalterable and that the children can do nothing to change this decision. The decision to divorce is an adult decision and is not a decision for the children to make. When the decision is made to divorce, let the children know that there will be no reuniting. Try to let your children know what to expect immediately as well as later on. Be as straightforward and realistic as you can be. Both parents are equally responsible for getting into a marriage, for the progress and process of a marriage, for the working out of problems that arise in marriage, and for the dissolution of a marriage if it continually fails to bring satisfaction to each partner. Too often the rights of children are ignored during the process of a divorce while the parents battle one another for a favorable position. Both parents are equally responsible for the well-being of their children. It is imperative for both parents to take this responsibility seriously and to do their part to assist their children.

Surviving the Divorce

Different people can help children cope with the psychological issues encountered when their parents make the decision to divorce. Parents, grandparents, special aunts and uncles, teachers, neighbors, religious instructors, and friends of the family have been the major influences on the emotional development of children. These individuals can continue to significantly impact the developmental process of most children as they go through the separation and divorce of their parents. Some children will need professional help when their parents divorce. This may be because of extreme difficulties in the divorce or because of the particular makeup of an individual child. It may also be a combination of both of these.

It is normal for children whose parents are divorcing to experience some negative short-term reactions such as anger, sadness, denial, fear, embarrassment or shame, and anxiety. These troubled reactions are greatest during the first year and will usually lessen by the second year following a divorce. It is the intensity and duration of these emotions that need to be considered in determining if you or your children need special help. Usually, you need to seek help for your child if physical symptoms develop or if there is a disruption in the normal day-to-day functioning of childhood. If there is a question in your mind about seeking help, consult a professional. Allow that person to be objective with you in evaluating your particular situation.

Some practical ways divorcing spouses can help their children is to let their children know they will always love them and will always be their parents. It is important to not talk badly about the other parent or other family member to the children. Keep your children out of the middle of disagreements you have with your former spouse. Never ask the children to take one side or the other. Encourage your children to spend time with the other parent. The healthier relationship children can have with both parents, the healthier the children will be.

Using the Professional Resources Available

There are many special mental health professionals who can help children and their parents through the divorce process. Some of the most readily available help can come from pediatricians, school counselors, principals, teachers, and school psychologists as well as religious leaders. Other mental health professionals with special training include psychologists, psychiatrists, counselors, social workers, pastoral workers, or family therapists (*All About Divorce,* see page 34).

When selecting someone to help you and your child, it is important to select someone who has experience in helping family members going through a divorce. It is equally important to find someone who has specialized training. Ask the people you trust for a recommendation. You'll be surprised by the number of resources available to you if you only ask. Make sure the individual you select is licensed or certified by the state department. Talk to the individual you are considering to make sure that you are comfortable with that professional and that you believe the person is most qualified. Take time to interview a few people before making a selection. Ask that professional for a referral if you believe you haven't selected the right person for yourself or for your children. A good fit is important in the counseling process.

"Research shows that in the years after a divorce, the most poorly adjusted children are those whose parents involve them in continuing conflicts. Children suffer when parents expose them to parental battles, when they criticize each other to the children, and when they fight through the children (*Helping Children Cope with Divorce,* see page 35).

"One of the strongest determinants of how well a child adjusts over the long run to divorce is whether the former spouses support each other in their continuing relationship as parents. Although this cooperation is essential for the child's secure adjustment, it is often difficult for parents to achieve" (*Helping Children Cope with Divorce,* see page 35).

If therapy is indicated, it will be important for both parents to be involved in the therapy for their children.

Knowing When to Seek Help

Be careful not to overlook significant changes in your children. Sometimes divorcing parents get so overwhelmed with their own problems that they neglect to see changes in their own children. Mary Blitzer Field in her book, *All About Divorce,* includes the following checklist. She suggests that you need to consult a mental health professional if you check even one of these statements.

☐ The child shows a pronounced loss of appetite, change of sleeping habits, or other disturbance in his day-to-day routine.

☐ The child seems angry or depressed all the time.

☐ The child has new difficulties in school, either socially or academically.

☐ The child is argumentative or defiant.

☐ The child wishes to be alone most of the time.

☐ The child displays constant physical symptoms including, but not limited to, stomachaches, tics, constant tiredness, aches and pains, headaches.

☐ The child has sudden mood swings.

☐ The child has a very negative view about everything and often says negative things about him/herself.

☐ The child shows an unusual degree of worry and anxiety.

Remember, knowing how to inform your children about your divorce, knowing what to expect both short term and long term from your children, and knowing when and how to select professional help can make a very painful time for parents less painful for their children.

PARENTING

Divorced Dads: Their Essential Influence

by Thomas W. Scott, M.S.

As often as we hear it, the word "divorce" still has the connotation of failure, ruptured dreams, legal entanglements, split allegiances. Betrayal, wounded women, philandering men. Who gets what, the end of traditions, moving out, moving in. Facing friends, family and public. Leaving old friends, learning how to make new ones, and so on and so on.

"Divorce" is a word that sends fear through a child's mind the same way the words "The Great Depression" sends horrific memories through the minds of the elderly.

When you hear the words, "Divorced Mother," you envision a woman thrown into a lifestyle and role that is not only taxing, but also totally unexpected, a woman experiencing a lonely, uphill battle.

But what do you think of when you hear the term "divorced dad"? Our society has a whole different way in which we envision the male end of the equation. Irresponsible, insensitive, abandoning. Hidden assets, self-centered, doesn't want to be bothered. Worthless, and, to some degree, a loser.

There is much men need to learn, not only about themselves, but also about the needs of their children. Following a divorce we don't have the choice of whether we can be a good husband, but we always have the choice to be a good father. I have learned more about divorced fathers in a one-hour session than their children have learned in their whole lifetimes. It's about time that men start to really understand the effects their absence has had on their child's emotional and developmental well-being and start to acknowledge the pain and emptiness they themselves have experienced from their own inability to parent in ways they had always hoped and dreamed of doing.

When a marriage ends and families split, you don't lose your children all at once; you lose them in pieces over a long period of time. Upon returning home from delivering the kids back to Mom, the silence can be very loud: A toy or doll that moments before had a life of its own lies motionless, the glass you insisted go in the dishwasher loses that urgency now when found in its same place, and folding little outfits that won't be worn for another two weeks emphasizes the solitude.

Just when you believe you've adjusted to the change, another particular missing part comes along and overwhelms you. The feeling that it will never be the same prevails. Then comes another day, and another missing part rears it thorny presence.

I can think of one case right off the bat of a nine-year-old girl whose mom and dad went through a bitter divorce. Her father, who possesses zero insight into himself and is totally disconnected to his own feelings and inner world, jumped into a rebound relationship with his daughter's day care provider. This wasn't premeditated, or ongoing prior to the divorce. It was more of a desperate attempt to bring someone in from the outside to make his insides feel better, thus distracting himself from his own loneliness and need to heal. It also created tremendous animosity between the woman and the mother, thus confusing the child further. It's been two or more years since this restructuring, and the father has since married this woman. The child tried to fit into this new family, but was not allowed to continue visitation due to reports of physical and verbal abuse at the hands of her previous care giver (the new wife). The father, who lives less than two minutes away on foot, has chosen not to see his daughter unless the stepmother is included. It has been over two years. So this little girl lives a life without a father, whose car she can see in his driveway whenever she passes by.

> **LEGAL TIP:**
> "Child snatching" is punishable by imprisonment in virtually every state and rarely does the party taking the child ever obtain legal custody.
> ■

This is one of the many pitiful stories and emotional histories children have experienced due to a father's inability to overcome a shallow and extremely wounded pride. Children value themselves to the degree they feel valued. They need continual reassurance that they are cared for and not forgotten. They need the message pounded home that "though we don't live together, it is very important for me to be with you."

I've had numerous children in my private practice express an extremely innocent and forlorn curiosity as to what dad is thinking, what he is feeling, what dad is doing, what he is eating, whom he is seeing. Security comes with knowledge and awareness. The more the child knows about you and your feelings, the more secure he will be.

You always hear about father-daughter, father-son bonding. That doesn't mean providing the child with an inexhaustible cornucopia of videos, lessons, treats and such. The things that are important to children are the things that cannot be repossessed, stolen or burnt. Bonding simply means sharing feelings. This is extremely threatening to some men. They believe the more they show, the more vulnerable they become. This might be true in the world of superficial relations, but it's not applicable, and very damaging, to a child. The physical absence that occurs through death, divorce or separation is painful and confusing enough to a child, but when coupled with the emotional abandonment, it creates a deep internal rupturing of the spirit, and no matter how much love other people bestow upon the child, it will never compensate.

Children quite often give fathers properties they don't possess in order to feel safe or loved. These are called "fantasy bonds," which are rooted in avoidance, thus creating the cycle of denial. What's sad is that this denial often spills over into numerous other areas of the child's life. When a father doesn't call, show up for visitations, or express much of an interest in the child's life, the child has a tendency to internalize this pain. Children don't ask themselves "what's wrong with him," but "what's wrong with me." I have often heard children say that they pretended things were fine, in order not to expose their pain and fragility. A false self is then constructed. Wearing defensive masks and becoming good little actors and actresses becomes a way of life. If mom is sad and depressed or – to the other extreme – if mom has never been happier, has lost weight, is dating, and displaying a new-found freedom that didn't exist within the marriage, children often feel that they are expected to be as happy as mom. I've had numerous women tell me how their children are sabotaging their new relationship. "All they do is just sit around depressed. They should be happy." In saying such things these parents discount the child's need to adjust and mourn.

Mothers have had to go far beyond the call of duty to compensate for their former mate's neglect. Due to their distorted perception of what's masculine and what is simply being human, men have missed out on the most rewarding privilege of life, parenthood, being a father, a daddy, a pop. I've heard it said, "Men can produce children, but few can be true fathers." True masculinity is often the opposite of everything that men have been taught. Thousands of men are finally willing to stop denying that they are in pain. Men have begun to listen to the hurts that run through their bodies like blood. The loss of the ability to parent in the ways men have always dreamed of is something that needs to be neutralized daily by spiritual growth, physical movement and contact with our children – not food, drugs, alcohol, work and women. For years I have called my children almost every day. Sometimes we talk for 20 minutes, other times for 30 seconds. But what they do know is that at the time of the call, they were in my heart and mind. This is also very rewarding to me, in that I really lose a sense of balance when a couple of days pass without hearing their voices. My sons and I often give each other hugs over the phone by saying "mmmmmmm." It feels very real to hear it back.

It is mandatory to acknowledge the pain and sense of loss experienced from the inability to tuck your kids in at night, read them stories, see them wander downstairs in their pajamas every morning, drop them off at school, help them put toothpaste on their brushes, open the lid on tight jars, go over their homework with them, and a multitude of other interactions that live-in fathers take for granted, or view as begrudging obligations. They are this age only once. Developmental stages are not something you can put on hold and get back to later when you have more time or are a little more secure. There is no hitting the rewind.

When I see the way fathers let their child's smiles go unnoticed, their scratches go unkissed and their voices unheard, I want to run over to the father and say, "Please pay attention." I'll never forget the time my 4-year-old son walked out of the kitchen saying, "In a minute, in a minute, in a minute." It really made me aware of the exasperation children feel when they are not being listened to.

Another example is the time my daughter ran over to me and asked me to tie her shoe. I looked up at her and said, "Don't you think you're old enough to tie your own shoe?" She was about 10 and had been tying her shoes for more than 7 years. Then I thought to myself, not only is it rare that she would make such a request, but she may never ask me to do so again. So I looked up at her and acknowledged this rare moment and said, "Honey, I'd love to." Her face beamed and for a wonderful moment she was a dependent little girl again.

Without a deep trust in our true masculinity and the maternal instincts men so often hide or deny, a man will often need a woman so much that she becomes his soul sustenance. He then finds it hard to derive the same degree of deep soulful love that being with his child can offer. Until men learn to deepen their ability to emote and be authentic with their kids, they will not be able to give and receive emotions of any real value.

Men need to retain some of the dignity that they feel has been ripped away by their ex-wives, the courts and the pain of living alone. In fact, men oftentimes cannot stand the solitude for very long. But when a man is wounded and still in a lot of pain he doesn't attract healthy women and vice versa. If we can give our children the time and the attention they deserve, these voids can be filled with a solid sense of self-respect, as opposed to another person's temporary adulation and pity.

> **LEGAL TIP:**
> In a few states, grandparents can get visitation rights with their grandchildren in addition to the visitation given to the non-custodial parent. This is true in Kansas and Missouri.

SURVIVING DIVORCE

What to Look for in the Child Care Industry

by Karen Clayton

More than 60% of young children in two-parent families have both parents in the workforce; with single-parent families the percentage is much higher. When parents face a divorce, they often must change their child care arrangements or begin using child care for the first time. A child easily spends ten or more hours a day in child care, making the responsibility of obtaining the best care possible a great concern for all parents.

Choosing Child Care

When parents are divorcing, their living arrangements change. While the best situation for a child whose parents are divorcing would be to minimize change by staying in the care arrangement he or she is in currently, this is often simply not possible. A stay-at-home mom may find that she needs to get a full-time job. If neither parent stays in the current home, new child care in a different area may need to be located. Income that used to support one family may now have to support two households, making the cost of child care a bigger issue. These concerns, added to the already stressful issue of looking for child care that is accessible, affordable, and dependable, and that provides safe, high-quality care may make the task of choosing child care seem overwhelming to parents in an already tough position.

Child care resource and referral agencies are able to help in a number of ways. Phone counselors can talk with parents about their different child care options, such as family child care, center care, or a nanny (relative care – care provided by a member of the child's family, such as a grandparent or aunt – is an option in many situations, but is something the parent usually works out on his/her own). They can describe each type of care, talk about costs of each option, and actually give names, addresses, and phone numbers of child care centers or people who do child care in their homes. Also, the phone counselors can give both verbal and printed information on the kinds of things parents should look for and think about when they're choosing child care.

The Child Care Association recommends that any parent looking for care should:

- **Explore the possibilities.** Choosing the right child care includes knowing the options of care available to you.

- **Think about your own preference** in the care of your child. Group size, flexibility in scheduling, ages of other children in the group, back-up care arrangements, etc., are things to think about.

- **Visit with prospective providers** by telephone and with a personal interview in the home or center. Observe how the provider interacts with the children in care. Ask to see the state license or registration. (Missouri providers may not have one.) Ask for references and follow up on them.

- **Choose your provider carefully.**
  If you have questions about child care regulations in general or child care business practices, consult either a Resource and Referral (R&R) agency or your local health department.
- **Follow up** with at least one drop-in visit after care begins to verify all is going well and your child is happy. Be sure to keep communication lines open with your provider.

Other things to look for and ask about when you visit a family child care home or a center should be listed in your R&R's brochure, or can be discussed with a referral counselor.

Financial Assistance

The cost of child care varies greatly. Don't assume that you have to choose the most expensive care to get the highest quality care. Location or the number of children in a home may influence the cost of care, but it does not mean that the care provided is superior to that provided in a home in a different area or with a couple of more children in care (but still within licensing regulations).

If you need assistance with child care expenses, Social and Rehabilitation Services (SRS) in Kansas or the Department of Family Services (DFS) in Missouri may be able to help. Your R&R may be able to suggest other programs that offer financial health. Also, some centers have sliding fee scales based on income. Ask the center director if that option is available.

The Provider or Caregiver

Parents often seem to go to one extreme or the other when involving their child care provider in their divorce. On one end of the spectrum is the parent who doesn't mention a word about what is going on at home. Unfortunately, these parents assume that their children will exhibit no outward signs that there is suddenly a big change in their lives. The short-term embarrassment experienced by a parent in sitting down for a few minutes to explain briefly that a divorce is taking place is minimal in comparison to the benefit of the awareness it provides the family child care provider or center teacher. What was strange or inappropriate or problem behavior quickly becomes understandable behavior when a caregiver knows what's behind a behavior.

At the other end is the parent who tries to involve the caregiver in every aspect of the divorce. Often one parent wants to enlist the caregiver in his or her fight with the other parent. They encourage the caregiver to report negatively on the other parent – was the child clean, fed, happy, etc., when she dropped her off this morning? Was the new girlfriend with him when he picked her up yesterday? If custody is shared, the caregiver may often see both parents and be asked to report both ways. They may be asked to give messages – some appropriate ("This is the number where she can reach me during the day tomorrow"), and some not so appropriate ("If she's just going to let him watch television all weekend while she works at home, tell her I'll keep him with me"). Providers need to be the child's teacher, not the parents' referee.

The best situation seems to be one where the caregiver knows the situation at home, without too many details. His/her main concern is the care and education of the child. One thing the caregiver always needs to know is who will pick the child up at the end of the day, whether it's mom or dad or grandma or older brother. Children need to know what's going to happen each day, so if custody arrangements mean that mom has the child three days and every other weekend and dad has him two weekdays and every other weekend, but sometimes days are traded or mom has a late meeting so someone else will pick him up, let the child know ahead of time! Last-minute changes or surprises can be extremely unsettling to any child, but especially to one facing other changes in his life. Again, let your child's caregiver be your partner in trying to do what's best for your child.

SURVIVING DIVORCE

Resource Listing

CHILD CARE INFORMATION

**Child Care Association
of Johnson County**
913/341-6200

Child Care Source
Kansas City Metro Area
913/573-CARE

Nannies of Kansas City Ltd.
913/341-6447

CHILD SUPPORT INFORMATION

Kansas

Olathe SRS Office
913/768-3300

Missouri

**State of Missouri
Child Support Enforcement**
816/889-5110
816/325-5820

COUNSELING

**Catholic Charities
Counseling Services**
Kansas
913/621-5058 or 800/227-3002

Communication Skills Center
Kansas City, MO
816/444-7771

Heart of America Family Services
Kansas 913/342-1110
Missouri 816/753-5280

**Jude La Claire
Life Weaving Institute**
Kansas City, MO
816/649-4803

Midwest Psychiatric Clinics
Overland Park, KS
913/345-1191

Lois A. Miller
Mission, KS
913/831-0009

**Connie Russell
Centerpoint Counseling
and Recovery**
Kansas City, MO
816/444-5511

**Tom Scott
Responsive Centers for
Psychology and Learning**
Overland Park, KS
913/451-8550

Prairie Center
Counseling & Mediation

Elizabeth J. Graham, LPC, NCC

601 N. Mur-Len
The Courtyard, Suite 12-B
Olathe, KS 66062

913/780-4777
fax 913/780-2436
eigraham@sound.net

Compassionate professional help for families dealing with divorce.
Call 342-1110.

Five convenient metro area locations. Sliding scale fee.

**Counseling Services
621-5058 or
1-800-227-3002**

Offices in Johnson, Wyandotte, Leavenworth, Miami and Douglas Counties

*JCAHO Accredited
Sliding Scale – Insurance Accepted*

**TRI-COUNTY
MENTAL HEALTH
SERVICES, INC.**

3100 N.E. 83rd Street, Suite 1001
Kansas City, MO 64119
(816) 468-0400 • http://www.tri-countymhs.org

When you need help, know where to turn.

EMOTIONAL/PARENTING - RESOURCE LISTING

Barbara C. Thompson
Professional Psychological
Institute
Kansas City, MO
816/756-3552

Tri-County Mental Health Services
Kansas City, MO
816/468-0400

Katherine White
White Professional Services
Kansas City, MO
816/756-3552

Raymore, MO
816/331-5888

COUNSELING AND MEDIATION SERVICES

Elizabeth Graham
Prairie Center Counseling
and Mediation
Olathe, KS
913/780-4777

Diane D. Lund
Kansas City, MO
816/931-0011

MISC/REFERRAL SERVICES

Abuse Hotline
816/995-1000

ADD/ADHD Education and Resource Association
913/362-6108

Alcoholic Anonymous Area Information Central Office
816/471-7229

Al-Anon/Alateen
816/373-8566

Counseling/Financial Assistance
816/621-1504

Johnson County Family Life Resources
913/262-9037

Mental Health Association of the Heartland
KC Area Support Group Listings
Help Line 913/281-1234

Safehome Inc. – 24 hr. Crisis Line
913/262-2868

Teen Hotline
816/281-2299

ORGANIZATIONS

Academy of Family Mediators
781/674-2663

American Arbitration Association
212/484-4100

Association of Family and Conciliation Courts
608/251-4001

Children's Rights Council
202/547-6227

Committee for Mother and Child Rights
540/722-3652

Midwest Psychiatric Clinics

James G. Hunter, MD & Associates

913/345-1191

James G. Hunter, M.D.
*Medical Director
Board Certified Child,
Adolescent & Adult
Psychiatrist*

Specializing in the evaluation and treatment of children, adolescents, adults and families.

- Adolescent issues
- Parenting concerns
- Crisis intervention
- ADD/ADHD/LD
- Alcohol & substance abuse
- Mediation
- Couples/family therapy
- Divorce recovery
- Depression & mood disorders
- Anxiety disorders

5350 College Boulevard, Suite 205
110th and Nall
in the College Corporate Center
Overland Park, Kansas 66211-1633

Divorce Hurts.

Find help at DivorceCare.

DivorceCare is a special weekly seminar and support group for people who are separated or divorced.

Call today for more information.

492-7752

*Sponsored by
Christ Lutheran Church
Lenexa, KS*

SURVIVING DIVORCE

National Child Support Enforcement Association
202/624-8180

Parents Without Partners
800/637-7074

PERSONAL AND PROFESSIONAL COACHING

Jean Darby
Raytown, MO
816/353-3309
816/353-8440

Victoria J. Elliott
Gladstone, MO
816/741-1570

RECOMMENDED READING

All About Divorce –
Mary Blitzer Field

Chicken Soup for the Soul –
Jack Canfield and
Mark Victor Hansen

Codependent No More –
Melody Beattie

Coping: A Survival Manual for
Women Alone – Martha Yates

The Courage to Divorce – Susan
Gettleman and Janet Markowitz

Crazy Time – Surviving Divorce
and Building a New Life –
Abigail Trafford

The Dance of Intimacy –
Harriet G. Lerner, Ph.D.

Divorce Busting –
Michelle Wiener-Davis

Men Are From Mars, Women Are
From Venus – John Gray, Ph.D.

My Life Turned Upside Down
But I Turned It Rightside Up –
Mary Blitzer Field

The Season's of a Man's Life –
Daniel J. Levinson

When Your Family Falls Apart –
Diana Daniels Booher

Women in Transition –
Carol Kott Washburne

Johnson County Family Life Resources

We strengthen healthy families and support and empower hurting families through education and programs such as:

- Active Parenting
- Marriage Encounter
- Retrouvaille
- Separated/Divorced Sharing
- Single/Divorced Fellowship
- Beginning Experience Weekend
- New Beginnings Program
- Remarried Preparation
- Rainbows Grief Support for Children
- Tough Love

For more information call (913) 262-9037.

LOIS A. MILLER, LSCSW, LCSW
Psychotherapist

5939 Woodson
Mission, Kansas 66202
(913) 831-0009

Individual, Marital
Step Family Counseling
Adoption Home Studies

A Catholic Church Response
The Family Life Office
a resource for referral

Ken Greene, Director
816/756-1850

Northland Outreach
St. Pius X High School
Tuesdays, 7-9 p.m.

South Central Services
Christ the King Parish
Thursdays, 7-9 p.m.

Divorced & Separated Recovery Group
St. Mark Parish, Independence
Wednesdays, 7-9 p.m.

Contact: Flora Boldridge, LCSW, LPC
221-4377, extension 316

Group Facilitator: Rebecca Mathews

When You Hurt We Care!

Divorce Recovery
8-week class
Call Ann at 942-3272

Colonial Presbyterian Church 9500 Wornall Rd., KCMO

Communication Skills Center
7611 State Line, Suite 140
Kansas City, Missouri 64114
(816) 444-7771

Counseling and Mediation for
- Divorce Closure
- Conflict Resolution
- Building a New Life

EMOTIONAL/PARENTING – RESOURCE LISTING

RECOMMENDED READING FOR PARENTS

101 Ways to Be a Long Distance Super-Dad –
George Newman

The Boys and Girls Book About Divorce –
Richard Gardner

Children, Divorce and the Church – *Doug Adams*

Dear Dad... – *Lee Shapiro, J.D.*

Dinosaurs Divorce: A Guide for Changing Families – *Laurence Brown* and *Marc Brown*

Divorce Happens to the Nicest Kids – *Michael S. Prokop, M.E.d.*

The Divorced Parent: Success Strategies for Raising Your Children After Separation – *Stephanie Marston*

For the Sake of the Children – How to Share Your Children in Spite of Your Anger – *Kris Kline & Stephen Pew, Ph.D.*

Growing Up with Divorce: Helping Your Child Avoid Immediate and Later Emotional Problems – *Meil Kalter*

Helping Children Cope with Divorce – *Edward Teyber*

Helping Your Child Through Separation and Divorce – *Glenda Banks*

Impact of Divorce, Single Parenting and Stepparenting on Children – *Mavis Hetherington* and *Josephine Arasteh*

Joint Custody with a Jerk: Raising a Child with an Uncooperative Ex – *Julie A. Ross, Judy Corcoran*

The Kids' Book of Divorce – *Ed Rofes*

Marriage, Divorce and Children's Adjustment – *Robert E. Emery*

The Parent-Child Manual on Divorce – *Maria Sullivan*

Part Time Father – *Edith Atkin* and *Estelle Ruben*

When Your Child Needs Help: A Parent's Guide to Therapy for Children – *Norma Doft*

Victoria J. Elliott
Personal and Professional Coaching

5510 NE Antioch Road, Suite 198
Gladstone, MO 64119
(816) 741-1570
MyCoachVJE@aol.com

Want to regain your sense of self and achieve lasting happiness in your life? Overwhelmed by life and its many challenges? Coaching empowers you to be more than you are and fulfills your potential for success and happiness. We will work together towards the achievement of your goals, your needs and your visions. Contact me today for a complimentary coaching session and/or more information.

Together We Achieve

LIFE TRANSITION SUPPORT
Jean Darby

"Helping You Find Balance in Your Personal and Professional Life"

(816) 353-3309
(816) 353-8440
Pathfnderz@aol.com

7009 Hawthorne
Raytown, MO 64133

SUPPORT GROUPS / WORKSHOPS

Al-ANON Family Groups Information Center
816/373-8566

The Catholic Chancery Family Life Office
Kansas City, MO
816/756-1850

Christ Lutheran Church
Lenexa, KS
913/492-7752

Christ the King Catholic Church
Kansas City MO
816/363-4888 or
816/221-4377 ext. 316

SURVIVING DIVORCE

Colonial Presbyterian Church
Kansas City, MO
816/942-3272

Emmanuel Baptist Church
Overland Park, KS
913/649-0900

First Baptist Church
Independence, MO
816/252-3377

First Baptist Church
Raytown, MO
816/353-1994

Jewish Family and Children's Services
Kansas 913/491-4357
Missouri 816/333-1172

Kid's Voice
Johnson County CASA Inc.
913/397-0322

St. Mark Parish
Independence, MO
816/221-4377 ext. 316

St. Pius X
Northland Outreach
816/221-4377 ext. 316

Queen of the Holy Rosary
Overland Park, KS
913/432-4616

Village Presbyterian Church
Prairie Village, KS
913/262-4200

Young Adult Beginning Experience (ages 16 - 25)
816/796-8711

What to Expect From the Legal Side

The Divorce Proceedings 38
Finding a Lawyer in Kansas City 40
The Importance of Communication 43
Attorney's Fees and Costs 45
Divorce in Missouri and Kansas:
Differences and Similarities 47
Resource Listing 52

Contributing Writers

LEGAL TIPS: ***MICHAEL J. ALBANO*** has been a member of Welch, Martin, Albano & Manners since 1968 and limits his practice to family law matters. Mike has spoken throughout the country on the issue of family law and is a published author of several articles in the field. He has been cited by numerous publications as one of the best matrimonial lawyers in the U.S. and has been named as one of "The Best Lawyers in America" in all editions of that publication. Mike is past president of The American Academy of Matrimonial Lawyers, Past Chairman of the American Bar Association Section of Family Lawyers and a diplomat of the College of Family Trial Lawyers.

FRANK B.W. "BILL" McCOLLUM and ***DANA L. PARKS*** are partners in the firm McCollum, Parks & Wilson, L.C. Bill graduated from Duke Law School in 1970. He was a member of the firm Spencer Fane Britt & Brown until 1991, when he became a principal in Holman McCollum & Hansen. In early 1998, Bill and Dana, along with Nancy Wilson, established McCollum, Parks & Wilson. Bill practices family, employment law and civil litigation in federal and state courts in Missouri and Kansas. Dana graduated from Washburn Law School in 1987. Dana limits her practice to family law. She handles divorces, custody/visitation matters, and post-divorce modifications. She is an active member of Kansas City, Missouri and Johnson County Bar family law committees. Their firm focuses on creative problem solving.

THE AMERICAN ACADEMY OF MATRIMONIAL LAWYERS was founded to improve the practice of law and the administration of justice in the area of divorce and family law. A small group of nationally known lawyers founded the Academy in recognition of the need to humanize and dignify this most traumatic area of family relations. The group's stated purpose: "To encourage the study, improve the practice, elevate the standards and advance the cause of matrimonial law, to the end that the welfare of the family and society be preserved." Fellowship in the AAML represents both a recognition of achievement in family law and a commitment to the highest standards of practice in that field.

Excerpts taken from the Divorce Manual – "A Client Handbook" published by the American Academy of Matrimonial Lawyers.

SURVIVING DIVORCE

The Divorce Proceedings

The goal of the legal process of divorce is to end the marriage and decide such issues as child custody, visitation, child support, alimony (sometimes called spousal support or maintenance), property and debt division and attorney's fees and costs.

A divorce judgment can be based on an agreement between the parties or result from a trial. An agreement is usually less traumatic for you and your children and less expensive than a trial. Ultimately, most cases are resolved without a trial.

- **The Petition:** A divorce begins with the Petition, called a Complaint in some states. This document notifies the court and your spouse, when served, that you want the court to end your marriage. It also lists what you are asking for, such as child custody, child visitation, child support, spousal support, property division, attorney's fees and costs.

- **The Response:** After a Petition is served, the other spouse is entitled to file opposing papers. In most states, if you are served with a Petition or a Complaint, you must file your opposing papers within a certain time or you will lose your right to present your side of the case to the court, and the court might give your spouse everything asked for in the Petition.

- **Temporary Orders:** Temporary orders, also called pendente lite orders, set the rules while the case is pending. Either party can ask the court to make temporary orders stating, for example, who stays in the house, who is responsible for the children, who pays which bills and the restraint of inappropriate conduct. It is best to agree upon reasonable arrangements while the case is pending rather than incur additional legal fees and add to bad feelings by having to go to court for temporary orders.

- **Discovery:** Each spouse is entitled to information from the other about the case. The legal procedure for obtaining that information is called discovery. Discovery may be a simple, speedy process or one consuming a great deal of time, energy and money.

There are several different discovery procedures, sometimes referred to as discovery devices. A list of questions known as interrogatories, requiring a formal written answer to each question, may be sent. By a request for production one party may obtain documents from the other. In a deposition, or examination before trial, the spouses and other persons, including experts, may be required to answer questions under oath in a lawyer's office while a court reporter takes down what is said and then prepares a transcript. If your deposition is to be taken, there will be advance notice and your lawyer will discuss the procedure with you.

Discovery may be conducted informally. It is often more efficient and less expensive for lawyers to informally exchange documents and information than to send and respond to

LEGAL TIP:
Divorce decrees are generally enforceable by contempt proceedings, attachment of property or garnishment.

LEGAL

interrogatories and requests for production and to take depositions.

- **Negotiated Settlement:** Most lawyers and judges agree that it is better to resolve a case by agreement than to have a trial in which the judge decides the outcome. Also, people who have been through a divorce value the privacy and control that a negotiated agreement gives them. People are more likely to obey a judgment which is based on their agreement than one which has been imposed by a judge. Voluntary compliance is important because enforcement procedures available from the court are usually expensive and sometimes inadequate. For these reasons, following discovery – and at any time, even during trial – the spouses and their lawyers should try to negotiate a settlement.

Because of the limited number of judges available to hear trials, most courts require the parties and their lawyers to attend a settlement conference in which a judge or other person tries to bring about a settlement. It is often very persuasive to hear from a judge how the judge would likely rule if the case went to trail. Although your lawyer may recommend that you accept or reject a particular settlement proposal, the decision to settle or not to settle is yours. Your lawyer cannot and will not make that decision for you. Even if the case is settled by agreement and you never see the inside of the courthouse, there are certain legal procedures that have to be followed to turn your agreement into a judgment and end your marriage. Your lawyer will complete this part of the process.

- **Trial:** If you and your spouse cannot settle your case, it will go to trial. At trial you each tell your story to the judge. It is told through your testimony, the testimony of other witnesses, and documents called exhibits.

Trial is likely to be expensive and unpleasant. However, it can be the only alternative to never-ending, unreasonable settlement demands. Still, trials are risky. No lawyer can predict the outcome of a trial because every case is different. A judge, a stranger – possibly with a viewpoint, temperament and values very different from yours – tells you and your spouse how to reorder your lives, divides your income and assets, and dictates when each of you can see your children.

Sometimes a trial does not end the case. Each party may, within a limited period of time, appeal to a higher court. An appeal adds more time and expense to the divorce process and is hard to win.

Advisory Board Member Note:

Individuals – especially women – tend to believe that the "expert" (lawyer or accountant) will take the responsibility for knowing what is best for them. That is *not true*. If you haven't taken that responsibility before you *must* in this case. You need to advise your attorney about your needs and desires rather than waiting for him/her to come up with the plan for your life, finances, children, etc. Experts are experts in their own fields – not in how your life should best be lived.

Carla Shelton Everhart
President, United Way of Wyandotte County

Excerpts taken from the Divorce Manual – "A Client Handbook" published by the American Academy of Matrimonial Lawyers.

SURVIVING DIVORCE

Finding a Lawyer in Kansas City

Selecting a lawyer to represent you in your divorce is more than just picking a name; it means establishing a close and sensitive relationship that will continue for months and perhaps years. It is important to find and hire the person who is right for you and your case.

Your state bar may have a process for certifying family law specialists and may give you names (see page 53). While certification is no assurance of quality, it usually requires a certain proven level of experience, study, and interest in the field. Certified specialists have usually passed an examination in this area of the law. The American Academy of Matrimonial Lawyers is an organization with a rigorous screening procedure which admits only qualified specialists.

Different things are important to different people when they are asking for names of lawyers, when interviewing lawyers and when deciding which lawyer to hire. For example, a person of limited means may be most concerned about cost. Another person may require experience with a certain type of family law problem. Decide what is important to you and select accordingly. Consider the following criteria:

- **Cost** – While local market conditions such as supply, demand, and competition determine in large part what lawyers charge, there can be a significant variation in fees. Generally, better known, better established lawyers charge more. The quality of representation you get may or may not be worth the higher price they charge. There are often highly skilled and experienced lawyers who charge less because they are not as well known and are therefore not in such demand. A lawyer in this category can be an excellent value.

  Even if cost is very important to you, don't reject a referral because you are told that a lawyer charges for a first consultation. Although some lawyers may give useful information and advice in a free consultation, there is a chance that a lawyer who is not charging for the time will treat the meeting more as a sales session and not feel obligated to deal with substantive issues. Even if your purpose is to interview the lawyer in order to help you decide whom to hire, you will not learn enough about the lawyer unless you talk about your case and hear what the lawyer really thinks about it.

- **Gender, age, race, religion and national origin** – Competent lawyers come in all sizes, shapes, genders, colors, religions and ages. None of these factors has anything to do with the lawyer's ability. Irrespective of the lawyer's ability, your comfort level is important if the relationship is to work. Hiring a lawyer with whom you share a common background or interest is acceptable as long as you are not being swayed by stereotypes.

- **Credentials** – There are objective factors that may help you evaluate the lawyer's professional competence and appropriateness for your case. Although mere membership in professional organizations may not mean a lot, active participation in the work of the organization is one mark of a lawyer's involvement in the specialty. Publishing articles, books, and treatises on family law and teaching other lawyers are even better indicators of experience, competence and reputation. The length of time in practice, and the amount of practice in family law are also important criteria.

- **Personal compatibility** – You must be comfortable with the lawyer you hire if you are to work effectively together. If you are not comfortable with a lawyer you interview, you should probably trust your instinct and not hire that person, even if you cannot isolate the cause of your discomfort. The relationship between lawyer and client in a family law matter is especially important. You will be telling the lawyer intimate facts of your life and the lawyer may have to give you advice and information that you may not like. Be sure the lawyer is one to whom you can talk and listen.

- **Location** – The location of the lawyer's office may or may not be important, depending on the circumstances. Here are some things to consider. It is a benefit to go conveniently to your lawyer's office to meet and work on your case. And if the lawyer's office is far from the courthouse, you may have to pay for the lawyer's travel time. On the other hand, lawyers sometimes represent clients who have never seen the lawyer's office, especially in large, sparsely populated areas where it is common for the lawyer to travel long distances to court, to depositions, and to meetings.

Interviewing

Many people hire the first lawyer they meet. Others interview several lawyers before deciding which one to hire. How many you interview may depend on how much time you have, the urgency of your situation, how many lawyers there are to choose from and how quickly you find one you like.

Tell the lawyer about your situation. Take a list of your assets and debts and sources of income with you. A copy of the last several years' tax returns can also help speed the discussion and make it more meaningful. A narrative or outline of the important events in your relationship with your spouse can also be helpful.

Make a list of things you want to discuss and take it with you to the interview. Ask questions. Then ask more questions. Listen carefully to the answers and write them down. Review the answers later and think about them. Listen not only to the information the lawyer gives you, but also to the way it was presented. Think about how the lawyer related to you. While a lawyer may be appropriately optimistic about your case, do not hire a lawyer simply because that lawyer predicts a better outcome than another lawyer. Here are some questions you might ask:

- What is likely to happen to me?
- How much property will I get?
- How much support will I get?
- How much support will I have to pay?
- Do I have a choice of courts?
- Does it make a difference?
- Do you have an associate or a paralegal?

> **LEGAL TIP:**
> Custody, support and permanent alimony can generally be modified following a final decree but laws vary widely on this.

- How do you decide who does what work on my case?
- Are you reachable by phone?
- If I call and you aren't available, how is my call handled?
- How much do you charge for travel time, secretarial time, photocopies, postage, faxes, long-distance calls, mobile phone calls, supplies, computer use or anything else other than your time?
- What expenses do you pay from the money I pay you and what do I have to pay directly?
- Under what circumstances would you refund all or part of my retainer fee?
- Do you have any personal feelings about the positions you would have to take if you represented me?
- How often are you out of the office in court, at conventions, on vacation, and for other things?
- How do you cover my case at those times?
- How much do you know about the judge who will decide my case if it goes to trial?
- Do you think we can work together?
- Will you be available at the times that are convenient for me?

Excerpts taken from the Divorce Manual – "A Client Handbook" published by the American Academy of Matrimonial Lawyers.

The Importance of Communication

The lawyer-client relationship works best when the two of you are able to communicate not only about the facts of your case, but about your working relationship.

Information should flow both ways between you and your lawyer. Just as your lawyer should satisfy your need for information, you should provide your lawyer with all the information that your lawyer requests. Advice based on incorrect or incomplete facts may be worse than no advice at all.

If you do not understand the advice you are given, or find it hard to accept, tell your lawyer. If, for example, you do not understand why your lawyer is recommending that you accept or reject a particular settlement proposal, you should ask why the recommendation is being made. Only by giving your lawyer the opportunity to explain things will you know whether there is a real problem to be addressed.

Your lawyer will ask you for financial information, and perhaps ask you to fill out a questionnaire. Financial information includes income, expenses, assets, and liabilities. Your lawyer may also want to see papers such as income tax returns, paycheck stubs, statements of savings and investments, employee benefit statements, and papers regarding your debts. Your cooperation in getting this information to your lawyer, although time consuming, is essential to the proper preparation of your case.

Your lawyer may also ask you to prepare a history of your marriage which includes personal as well as financial information. Where the custody of your children is in dispute, more than financial information will be necessary. In addition to a history, some lawyers ask their clients to keep a diary of events related to the divorce. Complete candor, including any negative facts about yourself, is crucial.

Your lawyer will be communicating with you. There may be periods of inactivity, but when something important happens, your lawyer will want to let you know. If you move, or are planning to be away, be sure your lawyer knows where you are.

Lawyers work on more than one case at a time and the practice of matrimonial law requires lawyers to spend time in court, at depositions, in conference, and on the telephone. So you should not expect your lawyer always to be available immediately when you call. You should, however, expect that your lawyer or a staff member, will respond to your telephone calls promptly. If an emergency arises, tell the person who answers the telephone that it is an emergency and explain the situation.

LEGAL TIP: If you have a joint passport, have a new one issued, for yourself and your children.

SURVIVING DIVORCE

Likewise, if your lawyer calls and leaves a message for you to call back, you should do so as soon as possible. Your lawyer will understand that you also have commitments that may make you temporarily unavailable. Your lawyer will appreciate your calling during regular business hours. However, most lawyers will make every effort to be available when needed for a real emergency.

You and your lawyer will have a hard time communicating if you are not available to each other. Before hiring any lawyer you should consider whether your schedules are compatible. If you can't meet with your lawyer during normal business hours, make that clear before you hire the lawyer. Remember that your lawyer is a human being, entitled to free time. If you expect your lawyer to be available evenings or weekends, say so in advance so that the lawyer can decide whether to take your case under those conditions.

Excerpts taken from the Divorce Manual – "A Client Handbook" published by the American Academy of Matrimonial Lawyers.

LEGAL

Attorney's Fees and Costs

It is important to both you and your lawyer that you talk about fees and costs at your initial conference. Unless fees and costs are discussed, either of you might make incorrect assumptions about what the other expects. False assumptions can lead to misunderstandings which can harm the lawyer-client relationship.

If you are concerned about the cost of your divorce, discuss with your lawyer how much you can afford to pay, how extensive the lawyer's work needs to be, and any limits you think should be placed on fees.

If you feel you can't afford the fees of the lawyer you consult, say so and ask for the names of other lawyers or agencies that can handle your case. You should make an agreement to pay fees only if you know you will be able to honor it.

Fees charged by lawyers vary from state to state and community to community. Some arrangements include:

- **Hourly Fee:** A fee based on the time expended and an hourly rate.

- **Retainer Fee:** A fee paid by the client to the lawyer to obtain a commitment from the lawyer to handle the client's case. A retainer can be a deposit against which the lawyer charges fees as they are earned. It can also be a non-refundable engagement fee. This is a fee that is sometimes charged by a lawyer for the agreement to take your case and to commit to being available for your case. Normally, an engagement fee is in addition to charges on an hourly rate basis. Your written fee agreement should specify whether a retainer fee is refundable, and if so, in what amount and under what circumstances.

- **Contingency Fee:** A percentage of the recovery. Contingent fees are generally forbidden in divorce cases but in some states are permitted in a proceeding to enforce the judgment.

- **Bonus (or results accomplished) Fee:** A fee based upon factors in addition to the hourly fee. Also called a premium or final fee.

- **Flat Fee:** A fee in a fixed amount for handling an entire case or a certain part of it.

- **Minimum Fee:** A fee which sets a floor on charges for services.

Fees are based on many factors, including the complexity of the case, the skill needed to perform the service properly, whether agreeing to represent you requires your lawyer to turn away other clients, the amount involved, the results obtained, the experience, reputation, and ability of your lawyer, the time limitations you impose, and the circumstances under which the services will be performed.

Your lawyer should ask you to sign a written fee agreement. You are entitled to an opportunity to review the fee agreement, to think about it, and to get answers to any questions you have about it.

SURVIVING DIVORCE

LEGAL TIP:

If you are in military service, you can generally avoid litigation under the Soldiers and Sailors Relief Act, but usually not in a divorce action.

■

You should read and understand it. Once you sign, the fee agreement is a legally binding and enforceable contract.

Different law offices have different procedures for handling costs and expenses. Those procedures are usually described in a written fee agreement. You may be responsible for paying out-of-pocket costs incurred for your case by your lawyer such as photocopies, postage, long-distance calls, court filing fees, process servers, court reporters, computer time and similar expenses. You will be responsible for paying any experts that you and your lawyer decide to hire. If you have questions about costs, ask your lawyer.

Your lawyer may ask you for security for payment of fees and costs in the form of a mortgage on your real estate or a lien on your property. You should carefully review and understand the security agreement and other papers. It is a good idea to review them with another lawyer before signing them. Similarly, your lawyer may ask you to have a friend or relative guarantee payment of your fees. Be sure that details are thoroughly discussed and that you and the guarantor both understand the papers before signing them.

Excerpts taken from the Divorce Manual – "A Client Handbook" published by the American Academy of Matrimonial Lawyers.

Divorce in Missouri and Kansas: Differences and Similarities

by Frank "Bill" McCollum and Dana Parks

There are differences and similarities in the divorce proceedings in Missouri and Kansas. This section gives an overview of the more significant differences and similarities. It goes without saying that it is important that you use a lawyer who is familiar with the laws and procedures in the state in which the divorce action is brought.

- **Divorce/Dissolution:** In Missouri, the proceeding to end a marriage is called a "dissolution of marriage" action. In Kansas, it is called a "divorce" action. Nevertheless, the ultimate result of either proceeding is the same – the marriage of the husband and wife is ended; custody and support of the children are set; spousal support is decided; and post-divorce ownership of property and responsibility for debts are determined. Throughout this publication the authors use the word "divorce" to mean the proceedings to end a marriage whether in Missouri or Kansas. The comments that follow, other than those relating to jurisdiction, generally do not apply if a valid pre-marital or post-marital agreement is in force. In that situation, the courts follow the terms of the agreement.

- **Jurisdiction:** The courts in Missouri and Kansas cannot decide a divorce case unless they have "jurisdiction" (i.e., power to decide) over at least one of the parties. In addition, a court cannot decide many issues unless it has jurisdiction over the other party, the parties' property and children. Usually if you, your spouse and children have resided in Missouri for 90 consecutive days, or in Kansas for 60 days, prior to filing, the court will have jurisdiction over all of the issues in a divorce action.

- **Temporary Orders:** When a divorce action is commenced, the courts in Missouri and Kansas can enter temporary orders. The orders are temporary because they are effective only until the court enters a final order for the financial support of you and your children. Though the courts are empowered to enter these orders, whether a court will do so is another matter. For example, when the petition for divorce is filed in Johnson County, Kansas, the court often immediately orders support to be paid and gives possession of the residence to one spouse and excludes the other spouse from even entering the residence. On the other hand, in Jackson County, Missouri, the judges are not likely to grant a request for such an order in a divorce action. It is important to note, however, that in Missouri if the spouse needing support has been abused or threatened, he or she may obtain temporary orders under the Adult Abuse Act. You do not need an attorney to obtain relief under the Act.

- **Maintenance (Alimony):** In those situations where the party seeking maintenance is employable, i.e., pre-retirement age and not disabled, the courts in Missouri are moving in the direction of granting only enough maintenance to allow a spouse to obtain the training which will lead to appropriate employment opportunities. In Johnson County, Kansas, on the other hand, the judges usually follow the maintenance formula set out in their guidelines. The guidelines set the amount of maintenance at 20% of the difference between the parties' gross incomes. They establish the period maintenance is paid as the first five years the parties have been married divided by 2.5, plus the additional years of the marriage divided by 3. Thus, a woman who has been married 29 years will receive maintenance for 10 years. Ten years of maintenance is the maximum the Kansas courts can order.

- **Child Support:** Procedures for setting child support are similar in Missouri and Kansas. Guidelines based on the gross income of the parents are used. The courts must follow them.

- **Child Custody:** The procedures for determining child custody and visitation are similar in Missouri and Kansas. There are two aspects of the custody of children: "legal" and "physical." "Joint legal custody" is the arrangement whereby both parents share decision-making rights, responsibilities and authority relating to the health, welfare and education of the child. This custody arrangement is preferred in both states over "sole custody." Physical custody denotes the child's primary residence. Very seldom does the court split physical custody. In determining legal and physical custody both states base the decision on "the best interests of the child." In order to determine those interests, the court looks at the circumstances of the parties and their children on a case-by-case basis. Your lawyer will tell you the factors the court will consider important in your situation.

- **Child Visitation:** Missouri and Kansas promote frequent contact between the child and the noncustodial parent. Even a parent who was previously uninvolved with the child is likely to get regular and frequent visitation unless there has been abuse or neglect of the child by that parent. Many counties in the Kansas City area on both sides of the state line have established guidelines for visitation. If one parent is designated the "residential" or "custodial" parent, the other parent is likely to obtain a standard visitation schedule consisting of every other weekend, some mid-week visitation and alternating holidays (but note that the Johnson County visitation schedule has a section that applies to infants and toddlers, which takes into account their special needs). Usually these schedules can be modified to reflect unique circumstances of the parents and the child. Missouri and Kansas both actively promote joint decision making and cooperation by the parents regarding visitation. Obviously, the courts would prefer that they work out their differences. In addition, Johnson and Wyandotte counties in Kansas and Jackson and Clay counties in Missouri require divorcing parents to attend parenting classes. Jackson County also requires children ages 6 to 17 of divorcing parents to attend a class.

If there are disputes relating to custody or visitation, Johnson and Jackson counties mandate mediation – a short-term, informal, non-therapeutic alternative resolution dispute process in which a neutral third party helps parties reach agreement (see page 53). Many other courts offer voluntary as opposed to mandatory mediation in custody/visitation disputes.

- **Property:** The courts in divorce proceedings address two primary issues with respect to property: Is the property marital or non-marital, and what is the fair market value of the property? The total value of all marital property is usually divided 50-50, absent egregious misconduct by one spouse. Frequently, the individual assets are not divided, rather they are given to one spouse or the other so that the value of all of the property a spouse receives is approximately equal to what the other receives. The non-marital property is not divided, but is set aside to the spouse who has the non-marital interest in it. In both Missouri and Kansas, gifts and inheritances received by one spouse from someone other than his or her spouse are generally considered non-marital property. Property that a spouse brings into the marriage (or is acquired with non-marital property) is also considered to be non-marital, but there are exceptions. One very important exception is that in Johnson County, Kansas, the increase in value (appreciation) of an asset that's non-marital is usually treated as marital property. Therefore, if you bring securities worth $100,000 into the marriage and they appreciate $50,000 between marriage and divorce, $100,000 is set aside to the owner while $50,000 is divided by the spouses. This is not the case in Missouri, where appreciation of non-marital property is also non-marital, so in the example, all of the stock is set aside to the person who brought it into the marriage.

- **Court Procedures:** The manner in which divorce cases are processed is similar in Missouri and Kansas. The case is assigned to a judge who makes the decisions. But there are procedural differences not only between the states but within each state. For example, Jackson County, Missouri, assigns cases to a "Family Court" where the judges handle only divorces and other family matters. Because so many cases are filed in Jackson County, it may take longer for the judge to act on your case, particularly if the case is contested, i.e., you and your spouse cannot agree as to how issues are to be resolved. In Kansas, and in other counties in Missouri, however, since the caseload is not as heavy, and divorce cases are not assigned to family court judges, your case may be processed more quickly than it would be in Jackson County.

Some of the courts in Missouri and Kansas adopt guidelines that the judges frequently, but not always, follow in setting child support and maintenance and dividing property. Ask your lawyer if the court has such guidelines and have her explain the guidelines that relate to your matter.

SURVIVING DIVORCE

IN THE CIRCUIT COURT OF JACKSON COUNTY, MISSOURI
AT KANSAS CITY

In Re the Marriage of   )
)
SS#   )
)
            Petitioner,   )   Case No. _____
)
and   )
)
SS#   )
)
            Respondent.   )

[PE]TITION FOR DISSOLUTION OF MARRIAGE

[N]ow Petitioner, _____, and for his/her
[petiti]on fo marriage states:

[Petiti]oner is and has been a resident of the State of
[in exc]ess of 90 days immediately preceding the filing
[and n]ow resides at _____, Kansas
[City, M]issouri.

[Respon]dent _____ is and has been a resident
[of Mis]souri for in excess of 90 days immediately
[precedin]g of this petition and now resides at
[in Kan]sas City, Jackson County, Missouri.

[Petitioner] is presently self-employed.

[Respondent] is presently employed by _____.

[Petitioner's] social security number is _____, and
[telephone] number _____.

6. Petitioner and Respondent were married _____, 19___,
in _____, Jackson County, Missouri, and said marriage is
registered in Jackson County, Missouri.

7. Irreconcilable differences have led to an irretrievable
breakdown in the marriage of Petitioner and Respondent; there is no
reasonable likelihood that the marriage of Petitioner and
Respondent can be preserved, and therefore, the marriage is
irretrievably broken.

8. ___ Children were born of the marriage of Petitioner and
Respondent, to wit: _____, born _____, 19___,
Social Security No. _____; and _____, born
_____, Social Security No. _____.

9. Petitioner is not now pregnant.

10. The children presently reside at _____, Jackson
County, Missouri, in the custody of the Petitioner and Respondent.
The best interest and welfare of the children will be served by
their legal custody being granted to Petitioner and Respondent and
their residential custody being granted to Petitioner.

11. Petitioner has not participated at any time in a[ny]
capacity in any other litigation concerning the custody of t[he]
children in this or any other state; nor does Petitioner kno[w of]
any custody proceeding that is pending in any court in this [state]
or any other state concerning the children; nor does Pet[itioner]
know of any person not a party to these proceedings [who has]
physical custody or who claims to have custody or visita[tion]
with respect to the children.

- 2 -

12. Petitioner is possessed of certain items of property which
are her separate property.

13. Petitioner and Respondent have accumulated property
during the course of the marriage, as well as certain obligations,
and Petitioner requests that the marital property and debts be
divided in a fair and equitable manner.

14. Neither Petitioner nor Respondent are members of the
Armed Forces of the United States.

15. Petitioner and Respondent are both over the age of 21.

WHEREFORE, Petitioner prays that the marriage of
_____ and _____ be dissolved, that legal
custody of the parties' minor children be awarded to Petitioner and
Respondent; that residential custody of the children be awarded to
Petitioner; that the Court order Respondent to pay a reasonable
amount to Petitioner for support of the parties' minor children,
that the Court set apart to each party his or her property and
divide the marital property in accordance with Section 451.330,
V.A.M.S.; that Petitioner be awarded a reasonable sum for her
maintenance and support; that Petitioner be awarded her attorney's
fees herein; and that the Court make such other orders as are just
and proper.

Sample: Divorce Petition

LEGAL

IN THE CIRCUIT COURT OF JACKSON COUNTY, MISSOURI
FAMILY COURT DIVISION AT KANSAS CITY

IN RE THE MARRIAGE OF)
)
Petitioner,) Case No. _____
)
and)
)
)
Respondent.)

DECREE OF DISSOLUTION OF MARRIAGE

Now on this _____ day of _____, 1996, come Petitioner/Wife/Husband in person and by her/his attorney, _____, and Respondent/Husband/Wife in person and by his/her attorney, _____.

This cause now coming on for hearing is submitted to the Court upon Petitioner's Petition for Dissolution of Marriage; and having heard the evidence, the Court finds:

1. That the Petitioner and Respondent have been resident of this state for ninety (90) days next preceding the commencement of this proceeding;

2. That thirty (30) days have elapsed since the filing of the Petition;

3. That neither Petitioner nor Respondent is a member of the Armed Forces of the United States of America on active duty;

4. That the Petitioner and Respondent were married _____ day of _____, 19___, said marriage being registered _____;

5. That the parties separated in _____;

6. That there was one child born of the marriage, namely _____, born October _____, 19___; who is now emancipated.

7. That Petitioner is not now pregnant;

8. That Petitioner resides at _____, Kansas City, Jackson County, Missouri; she is not employed; her Social Security number is _____.

9. That Respondent resides at _____, Kansas City, Jackson County, Missouri; he is employed by _____, Kansas City, Missouri; and his Social Security number is _____;

10. That the Petitioner and Respondent own non-marital property;

11. That the parties own marital property;

... ns no reasonable likelihood that the ... served; and, therefore, the ... ave entered into a Separation ... t that is not unconscionable, ... of the parties, including the ... and said Agreement further ... ssets and liabilities. The ... t forth in full)

WHEREFORE, IT IS ADJUDGED AND DECREED by the Court that the marriage heretofore existing between the Petitioner and Respondent is hereby dissolved.

IT IS FURTHER ORDERED AND ADJUDGED that the Court's order of _____, is rescinded and is no longer effective.

IT IS FURTHER ORDERED AND ADJUDGED that the court costs of this action be paid by the party who incurred the cost.

IT IS FURTHER ORDERED AND ADJUDGED that the parties perform the terms of their Separation Agreement and Property Settlement which is set forth in its entirety above.

IT IS SO ORDERED.

_____
Judge

APPROVED AS TO FORM:

_____ _____
Attorney for Petitioner Attorney for Respondent

Sample: Divorce Decree

SURVIVING DIVORCE

Resource Listing

AMERICAN ACADEMY OF MATRIMONIAL LAWYERS

THE AMERICAN ACADEMY OF MATRIMONIAL LAWYERS was founded to improve the practice of law and the administration of justice in the area of divorce and family law. The group's stated purpose: "To encourage the study, improve the practice, elevate the standards and advance the cause of matrimonial law, to the end that the welfare of the family and society be preserved."

Michael J. Albano
Independence, MO
816/836-8000

Regina Keelan Bass
Kansas City, MO
816/444-8030

Gail Berkowitz
Kansas City, MO
816/753-5000

Sheldon Bernstein
Kansas City, MO
816/444-8030

Daniel H. Bowers
Kansas City, MO
816/444-8030

Jerold A. Bressel
Overland Park, KS
913/498-1500

Micheline Z. Burger
Olathe, KS
913/829-9118

Jack Cochran
Blue Springs, MO
816/229-8121

James T. Cook
Kansas City, MO
816/753-5000

Karen M. De Luccie
Independence, MO
816/836-8000

John W. Dennis, Jr.
Independence, MO
816/836-8000

Gina M. Graham
Blue Springs, MO
816/229-8121

Elizabeth Hill
Leawood, KS
913/381-1500

John H. Johntz
Overland Park, KS
913/469-4100

Scott H. Kreamer
Olathe, KS
913/782-2350

R. Michael Latimer
Shawnee Mission, KS
913/789-7477

Donna M. Manning
Olathe, KS
913/829-2255

T. Bradley Manson
Overland Park, KS
913/498-8080

Michael C. McIntosh
Independence, MO
816/373-5590

Ronald Nelson
Overland Park, KS
913/469-5300

Joe L. Norton
Olathe, KS
913/782-2350

Thad E. Nugent
Overland Park, KS
913/338-0011

Karen A. Plax
Kansas City, MO
816/942-1900

Anita I. Rodarte
Kansas City, MO
816/444-8030

J. Bradley Short
Overland Park, KS
913/491-4400

James H. Young
Blue Springs, MO
816/228-3222

LEGAL – RESOURCE LISTING

ARBITRATION/MEDIATION SERVICES

**Jackson County Family Court –
Domestic Relations Services**
Kansas City, MO
816/881-6526

**Johnson County Office
of Court Services**
Olathe, KS
913/324-6900

Hugh F. O'Donnell III
Kansas City, MO
816/474-0003

**ElGene Ver Dught
Mediation Services of Missouri**
816/836-4141

**Wyandotte County Domestic Court
Services (Case Management)**
Kansas City, KS
913/573-2833

AREA BAR ASSOCIATIONS

Kansas Bar Association
913/233-4322

Kansas City Bar Association
816/221-9472

Missouri Bar Association
314/635-4128

LEGAL SERVICES

Kansas

Jerold Bressel
Overland Park, KS
913/498-1500

**Nancy Caviar
Caviar & Hill, L.C.**
Leawood, KS
913/381-1500

**Janet L. Damore
Schlagel, Damore & Gordon, LLC**
Olathe, KS
913/782-5885

**Jamee C. Fritzemeier
Schlagel, Damore & Gordon, LLC**
Olathe, KS
913/782-5885

DAVID P. KIMMINAU
ATTORNEY AT LAW

McELLIGOTT, EWAN, HALL & KIMMINAU
A PROFESSIONAL CORPORATION

(913) 648-6265
7199 WEST 98th TERR.
SUITE 130
OVERLAND PARK, KS 66212

(816) 833-1222
233 WEST WALNUT
INDEPENDENCE, MO 64050

HUGH F. O'DONNELL, III
ATTORNEY AT LAW
AND
FAMILY MEDIATION

2546 HOLMES
KANSAS CITY, MISSOURI 64108

OFFICE
(816) 474-0003

JANET L. DAMORE
ATTORNEY AT LAW

JAMEE C. FRITZEMEIER
ATTORNEY AT LAW

Schlagel Damore & Gordon, LLC
(913) 782-5885
Fax (913) 782-0123

128 S. Chestnut
P.O. Box 683
Olathe, KS 66051-0683

LAW OFFICES OF LINDA F. DYCUS
MATRIMONIAL LAW

LINDA F. DYCUS
SUZANNE E. DOHERTY

2623 HOLMES
KANSAS CITY, MISSOURI 64108

(816) 842-7600
(816) 842-3102 (FAX)
www.lfdycus@kcnet.com

Joseph A. McMillen

Attorney At Law
Divorce Mediator

7301 Mission Road, Suite #313
Prairie Village, Kansas 66208

Phone (913) 362-7122
Fax (913) 362-7423

PEARMAN & GALAMBA, L.C.
ATTORNEYS AT LAW

JAYNE A. PEARMAN
SUSAN SAPER GALAMBA
JOHNATHAN L. MEYER

9229 WARD PARKWAY, SUITE 107
KANSAS CITY, MISSOURI 64114

(816) 444-0003
FAX: (816) 444-0021

SURVIVING DIVORCE

David W. Hughes
Cashin & Hughes
Prairie Village, KS
913/362-7122

S.W "Woody" Longan, III
Longan & Associates
Leawood, KS
913/491-4050

T. Bradley Manson
Shapiro, Manson & Karbank
Overland Park, KS
913/498-8080

Joseph McMillen
Prairie Village, KS
913/362-7122

Thad E. Nugent
Overland Park, KS
913/338-0011

Keven M.P. O'Grady
Ferree, Bunn & O'Grady Chartered
Overland Park, KS
913/381-8180

Karen L. Shelor
Sexton, Shelor, Latimer & Pryor
Shawnee Mission, KS
913/789-7477

Missouri

Michael J. Albano
Welch, Martin, Albano & Manners
Independence, MO
816/836-8000

Linda F. Dycus
Suzanne E. Doherty
Kansas City, MO
816/842-7600

Susan Galamba
Pearman & Galamba
Kansas City, MO
816/444-0003

Major D. Hammett
Hammett & Schmidt, P.C.
Kansas City, MO
816/421-1521

Diana R. Howell
Kansas City, MO
816/751-0560

W. Geary Jaco
Kansas City, MO
816/221-4411

David P. Kimminau
McElligott, Ewan, Hall & Kimminau
Independence, MO
816/833-1222

Sharon R. Lowenstein
Kansas City, MO
816/751-0553

Frank B.W. McCollum
McCollum, Parks & Wilson, L.C.
Kansas City, MO
816/756-1114

Where should I turn for legal help regarding my divorce?

McCollum, Parks & Wilson

Frank B.W. "Bill" McCollum and Dana L. Parks are partners in the firm McCollum Parks & Wilson, L.C. Bill graduated from Duke Law School in 1970. He was a member of the firm Spencer Fane Britt & Brown until 1991, when he became a principal in Holman McCollum & Hansen. In early 1998 Bill and Dana along with Nancy Wilson established McCollum Parks & Wilson. Bill practices family, employment law and civil litigation in federal and state courts in Missouri and Kansas. Dana graduated from Washburn Law School in 1987. Dana limits her practice to family law. She handles divorces, custody/visitation matters, and post-divorce modifications. She is an active member of Kansas City, Missouri, and Johnson County Bar family law committees. Their firm focuses on creative problem solving.

For additional information or to schedule an appointment with Bill or Dana, call (816) 756-1114. We are located on the Country Club Plaza at Two Brush Creek Boulevard, Suite 425, Kansas City, Missouri 64112 *(Northeast corner of 47th and Main Streets).*

LEGAL – RESOURCE LISTING

Michael C. McIntosh
Schaffer, McIntosh & Effertz
Independence, MO
816/373-5590

Johnathan L. Meyer
Pearman & Galamba
Kansas City, MO
816/444-0003

Hugh F. O'Donnell III
Kansas City, MO
816/474-0003

Dana Parks
McCollum, Parks & Wilson, L.C.
Kansas City, MO
816/756-1114

Jayne A. Pearman
Pearman & Galamba
Kansas City, MO
816/444-0003

David Lee Wells
No. Kansas City, MO
816/842-2171

MISCELLANEOUS INFORMATION

JoCo District Attorney's Victim Assistance Unit
913/764-8484 ext. 5237

Legal Aid
913/764-8585

Metrowide Abuse Hotline
816/995-1000

Safehome Inc. – 24 hr. Crisis Line
913/262-2868

ORGANIZATIONS

American Academy of Matrimonial Lawyers
312/263-6477

American Arbitration Association
212/484-4100

Academy of Family Mediators
781/674-2663

Association of Family and Conciliation Courts
608/251-4001

The Father's Rights and Equality Exchange
415/853-6877

National Center on Women and Family Law
212/741-9480

National Child Support Enforcement Association
202/624-8180

National Congress for Fathers and Children
913/342-3860

National Women's Law Center
202/588-5180

NOW Legal Defense and Education Fund
212/925-6635

Women's Legal Defense Fund
202/986-2600

AGGRESSIVE DEFENSE

Law Offices of W. Geary Jaco

20+ Years of Trial Experience

Family Law
Se Habla Espanol

W. GEARY JACO • CHRISTOPHER J. ANGLES

1100 Main, Suite 1850

221-4411

Members: Natl. Assoc. of Criminal Defense Lawyers
MO Assoc. of Criminal Defense Lawyers
American Trial Lawyers Assoc.

Serving All of Missouri & Kansas • Admitted in 5 Federal Jurisdictions

---

Law Offices of
THAD E. NUGENT

Domestic and International Divorce
Complex Custody • International Custody

Fellow of the
International Academy of Matrimonial Lawyers and
American Academy of Matrimonial Lawyers

6900 College Blvd.
Overland Park, Kansas 66211

(913) 338-0011
Fax (913) 338-4483

Longan & Associates

Attorneys at Law

Our goal is to assist you through the legal process as economically and as quickly as possible.

S. W. Longan, III
Patricia L. Lear-Johnson
Leawood Executive Centre
4601 College Boulevard
Suite 140
Leawood, Kansas 66211
(913) 491-4050
FAX (913) 491-9318

SURVIVING DIVORCE

RECOMMENDED READING

A Guide to Divorce Mediation – *Gary Friedman*

Between Love and Hate – *Lois Gold*

The Complete Legal Guide to Marriage, Divorce, Custody and Living Together – *Steven M. Sack*

The Divorce Law Handbook: A Comprehensive Guide to Matrimonial Law – *Elliot D. Samuelson*

Divorce Yourself: The National No-Fault Divorce Kit – *Daniel Sitarz*

How to Get Your Uncontested Divorce: On Your Own and Without an Attorney – *Sherry Wells*

Practical Divorce Solutions: A Guidebook – *Charles E. Sherman*

A Woman's Guide to Divorce and Decision Making: A Supportive Workbook for Women Facing the Process of Divorce – *Christina Robertson*

DIANA R. HOWELL
ATTORNEY AT LAW

4505 MADISON AVENUE
KANSAS CITY, MISSOURI 64111

816•751•0560

FERREE, BUNN & O'GRADY
CHARTERED
9300 Metcalf Ave., Suite 300
Overland Park, Kansas 66212
(913)381-8180

*Divorce, Post-Divorce, Adoption
Pre-Marital Agreements
Estates and Probate*

Jerold A. Bressel
attorney at law

Fellow: American Academy of Matrimonial Lawyer
Licensed in Kansas and Missouri

DIVORCE • FAMILY LAW
BUSINESS/CORPORATE LAW
REAL ESTATE

10955 Lowell, Suite 720
Overland Park, KS 66210

498-1500

Free Initial Consultation

Financial Decisions: Making the Right Choices

*How to Navigate Through Divorce
and Build Financial Security* 58

Finding/Selling Your Home in Kansas City 62

Resource Listing 64

Contributing Writers

SANDI WEAVER'S goal is to help individuals successfully meet the difficulties of divorce and move toward a secure future. She is a member of the Missouri Society of CPAs, and has presented information on financial analysis in divorce to CPAs throughout the state.

Ms. Weaver holds the professional license of Certified Financial Planner. She is a member of the Heart of America chapter of the International Association of Certified Financial Planners, the local professional organization.

Ms. Weaver has been awarded the Chartered Financial Analyst designation, which is prevalent among professionals in the investment field. She is a member of the Association for Investment Management and Research, the professional organization for CFAs.

JEANETTE K. LEE has been successfully selling real estate in the Kansas City area since 1977 and is licensed in Kansas and Missouri with RE/MAX First Realtors. She has a Master's Degree in Education and also counseling certification. She is an Accredited Buyer Representative (ABR), Certified Residential Specialist (CRS), and Graduate Realtor Institute (GRI).

Jeanette is a highly respected professional among her peers. Her continued support of Children's Miracle Network, the corporate charity, has been greatly appreciated. Consistently a member of RE/MAX 100% Club, Jeanette attributes her success to continued referrals of past satisfied clients.

SURVIVING DIVORCE

How to Navigate Through Divorce and Build Financial Security

by Sandi Weaver

The path through divorce is filled with stumbling blocks. "I just want to hurry and get it over with!" is a common misstep. Please take time to analyze your financial position and make wise financial decisions. Divorce is painful, but ensuring your financial security is critical for your future.

During divorce both parties negotiate to divide the marital assets. Who gets the house? Who keeps the good car? According to law, you and your spouse should split the property in a fair and equitable manner. Your decisions are recorded in a formal document, the property settlement agreement. Use the following tips to plan ahead and avoid the common pitfalls we've helped others sidestep.

Watch out what you bargain for – you might get it

People are often determined to ask for the house when dividing the marital property. It's understandable. Before doing so, however, be sure to review the financial impact. Let's take a scenario with Mr. and Mrs. Smith who are divorcing. Mrs. Smith is bargaining to keep the house for the sake of their two children. Mr. Smith agrees. In return, he takes the savings account which equals the home's equity. One year later Mrs. Smith decides to sell the house. Her budget is just too tight. Unfortunately, Mrs. Smith may encounter three common pitfalls.

Houses seldom sell for the original estimated sales value. If the house sells for less than the value estimated back in the divorce, that shortfall comes right out of Mrs. Smith's equity. The loss is not shared with Mr. Smith. Secondly, Mrs. Smith will bear the costs of selling and moving alone. If the decision to sell the house had been made prior to divorce, those may have been shared expenses. Finally, Mrs. Smith will likely have damaged her financial position in the past year trying to keep up with the house payments. Some people accumulate dangerous amounts of credit card debt, trying to make the house payments. Some cut expenses drastically, eliminating clothing purchases, cable tv, and more, trying to make the house payments.

We see this difficult situation all too often. Take steps to protect yourself before you negotiate for the family home. Calculate your likely future financial position, the income and expenses. Are your housing costs within the 30% standard guidelines? If not, explore the alternatives which may let you keep the home without destroying your future financial security.

Look ahead to retirement

When you're preparing, review your retirement funds, the pension plans and IRAs. Consider carefully before deciding to trade other assets in order to keep your own retirement fund or to bargain for a portion of your spouse's. Here are four questions to answer.

What will you need money for? What are my future needs, both short-term and long-term? Prioritize your list. Many are faced with the need to purchase a new home or condo. You may need funds for training or higher education to support yourself. If your future budget is going to be somewhat tight, you may need additional investments for supplemental income.

What do I intend to do with the retirement fund? Pensions and IRAs are intended to meet your long-term goal for retirement, to generate income during the golden years. Pensions are not liquid assets or cash. Don't give up a savings account for pension assets if you'll need funds to purchase a new home or to finance education. If you face no major purchases and you'll be able to support your new lifestyle, go ahead and negotiate for those retirement funds and benefit from deferred taxes.

Will I need to withdraw money early from this retirement fund? Before bargaining for pension assets, know what direction you'll take with that asset. If you withdraw funds now for cash needs, without planning for it in your legal documents, you'll likely face three unpleasant consequences. First, the Internal Revenue Service assesses a penalty for early withdrawals from certain retirement funds. That penalty is based on the gross, not net, amount takeout. Second, money withdrawn from retirement funds is taxed under ordinary income rates, not the lower capital gains rates. Third, such lump-sum withdrawals can drive you up through the tax tables until you're paying at the very top rates, 39.6%. It's not uncommon for people to pay over 50¢ in penalties and taxes for every $1 taken. Plan ahead in your legal documents to minimize taxes and penalties if you'll need to withdraw money from retirement funds.

How much is it worth in cash? When bargaining to keep your own retirement fund or for a portion of your spouse's, determine how much the pension is really worth. Track down the cost basis and account for income taxes, surrender charges and redemption fees. If you're trading cash in the bank in order to keep this pension, be sure to use an equivalent basis – apples to apples.

LEGAL TIP:
Make sure you have the originals of deeds, notes, car titles and other documents which should be in your possession, and place them in a safe deposit box.

Track down details on the retirement funds being divided. If one of the pensions is yours as an employee, check if you can take out a loan from your account balance. That can be a valuable feature, particularly if you'll need cash for a house downpayment or other needs. Negotiate to keep that pension while perhaps giving up other retirement fund assets.

If you're bargaining for a portion of your spouse's pension, check the distribution rules for you as an alternate payee. Oftentimes, you'll have to wait for your benefits until your spouse decides to quit working, not when you decide you'll need that pension check. If so, see if the pension allows you to roll out your portion into an IRA where you'll have more control over when to take your benefits. If not, other retirement funds may be a better option.

Remember that not all pensions are concrete guarantees. Some plans may disappear in a corporate bankruptcy. Some pensions hold investments that have a questionable future, such as stock in a small, private company that may, or may not, be worth much when you retire.

Not all investments are alike

If you and your spouse have investments, such as a CD at the bank, a mutual fund, or stocks in a brokerage account, don't settle for a 50-50 split.

You can do better than that. This is a chance for both parties to reach a win-win solution. Before you begin negotiating, evaluate each investment based on its tax consequences, risk level, and the income versus growth potential.

What taxes would the Internal Revenue Service collect if the investment were sold? Don't trade $2,000 in a checking account for $2,000 in stocks. Investments that generate passive losses, such as tax shelter partnerships, are best paired with those that generate passive income.

Evaluate your earning capacity. If you have a high earnings capacity, you have a better ability to tolerate risky investments and earn potential greater returns. Safer, more conservative investments are more suited for those with a low earnings capability when investments cannot be easily replaced. Research each of your investments to determine the risk. Don't bargain for investments which will damage your financial security. You need assets which are appropriate for your future situation.

Analyze your future budget. What are your expenses likely to be? What income do you anticipate? Determine if you'll need to use investments to supplement your budget. Select investments that produce income rather than appreciation. For example, a bond normally throws off more cash, in the form of interest, than a stock pays in dividends. Choose investments that will form a properly balanced portfolio to earn solid returns, with a risk level that's appropriate for you.

Do you face major purchases or cash needs? Bargain for investments that can be sold easily at a fair price. A money market fund may be a better choice than a bank CD with withdrawal penalties. Selling shares of stock may consume fewer commission dollars than a mutual fund with a 5% redemption fee.

Put it in black and white

Be ready to provide your attorney with solid facts and figures. Thoroughly analyze your income and expenses to clearly and concisely state your case. Accurately show the standard of living in your marriage to ensure that any maintenance, or alimony, is adequate. If you're likely to pay support, you don't want those expenses overstated. If you're requesting maintenance, you don't want those expenses understated.

When analyzing your income and expenses, be sure to include all expenses. Review all canceled checks, credit card statements, and how you handle cash. If you miss a few expenses in the first month and similar expenses the next month, you'll likely omit a substantial chunk of expenses over an entire year.

It's important to be thorough when reporting income. Review tax returns, W-2 statements, employee benefit handbooks and statements to verify you've added up all the income. If you or your spouse own a business, you may need to add back travel and entertainment expenses, possibly non-cash expenses such as depreciation. Review your employee benefits statements for income. If an employer contributes to a spouse's pension, that can be income. Beware, not all employer contributions are reported on your 1099 or W-2 statements.

Identify any dissipation of the marital estate, where third parties have inappropriately received funds. Fully document your children's needs. Verify that the child support amounts you and your spouse are discussing will adequately support your children's needs. A thorough analysis of your income and expenses, though time-consuming, is vital for your future security and well worth the effort.

> **LEGAL TIP:**
> In some states a will becomes null and void after a divorce. This is true in Kansas and Missouri as to your ex-spouse only.
> ■

After it's over organize your finances to avoid future crises

You've been through enough. Get back to basics with a budget. Work through four steps. Use last year's income and expenses, which you've already analyzed, as a base. Then provide for known changes such as maintenance, child support, professional fees, counseling, etc. Third, adjust the budget for predicted changes, such as additional meals out or hiring out yardwork, which often arise as a result of divorce. In the last step balance anticipated expenses with income.

It's quite probable you'll need to cut low-priority, discretionary expenses. The same pot of money will not support two households as well as one. Consider making one or two major lifestyle changes to balance the entire budget. For example, drive an economy car and eliminate the lease on your high-end automobile. Review your tax situation to fully utilize all strategies to keep your tax bills low. Don't ignore the other side of the equation – income. If you're not employed, consider a full- or part-time position and open your horizons to new experiences. Focus on employment which provides benefits. Explore additional employment which requires little time or which you truly enjoy for extra income. Consider shifting investments to produce income to supplement your budget.

Finally, a potpourri

Adjust your W-4 withholding if you're paying maintenance. You'll have additional deductions. When you receive maintenance, be sure to file estimated payments for taxes with the Internal Revenue Service. Close all joint credit cards to eliminate late charges to the accounts. Review all insurance policies – auto, homeowners, medical, and life. If you were covered by your spouse's medical insurance, you'll likely be dropped. According to COBRA law, you have the right to continue that insurance for a short-term period by paying no more than 102% of the same group rate. Update beneficiary designations on insurance policies, annuities, IRA accounts, wills and trusts. Once the divorce is final, don't delay in transferring titles on the divided property to the appropriate spouse. Substantial delays can have severe consequences. File quit-claim deeds where appropriate to avoid claims by ex-spouses or their creditors. Obtain support documentation on property you received in the settlement. It'll be much easier to get the records now than in three years.

LEGAL TIP: Without a will, property which goes to your children will be controlled by your ex-spouse.

Adjust your investment plan and asset allocation since your investments have undoubtedly increased or decreased. If you received retirement funds in the settlement and are rolling the investments into your own IRA, follow sound investment planning guidelines. Readjust your investments based on your new financial position – you may need to lower your risk level. Build a savings fund for emergencies totaling three to six months of living expenses. Then rebuild your retirement funds using tax-deferred means such as IRAs and pension funds. If your employer provides matching contributions, participate and enjoy an immediate, windfall return on your savings.

Divorce is difficult and painful

Make wise financial decisions to ensure your financial security. Get sound financial advice when your situation calls for it. As others have said, this is an opportunity to start anew, but you don't have to start over.

SURVIVING DIVORCE

Finding/Selling Your Home in Kansas City

by Jeanette K. Lee

A home and its furnishings are the physical possessions that must be divided or sold. A home represents what is past. So what to do with that home, to keep it or sell it, becomes a major decision.

Jeanette K. Lee

Whatever decision you reach will largely determine the plan for your future. Therefore, sound professional real estate advice becomes very important to both future emotional and financial well-being.

Most women have very strong emotional attachments to their homes. The home is a woman's turf and, therefore, her territory to exercise the feminine nesting instinct. When a woman divorces, the home often becomes symbolic of the break-up.

Home to a man is more a balance sheet of assets and debits. He looks at it from an investment perspective more than the female.

If you think there is even the possibility that you will sell your home, seek professional real estate advice. The selection of a real estate agent is very important. Choose an agent who is upbeat, positive, patient, experienced and service-oriented. Also, a person in a divorced situation really needs an agent who is sympathetic and understanding as well as a good listener.

Once the selection of a real estate agent has been made, seek the agent's advice concerning the options available.

Here is a good list of questions:

1) **What is the house worth?**

A real estate agent can provide a comparative market analysis that shows homes currently on the market as well as recent sales. It may also be in your best interest to have a professional appraisal of the property which costs between $200-$300 and would probably be money well spent.

2) **How much does the house cost to maintain?**

What is the monthly payment? How much are insurance and taxes? Does the house need any immediate major repairs? What are the monthly operating expenses? If you are unaware of these figures, a professional real estate agent can assist you in finding answers to these questions and then help you determine if remaining in the home is an affordable option.

3) **How much will it cost to relocate?**

The real estate agent can provide information concerning selling costs, moving costs and buying costs.

FINANCIAL

4) If I decide to relocate, what can I afford to buy?

The experienced agent can tell you about homes in the local market that are in your projected price range. Should you be moving out of the Kansas City area, the agent can refer you to reputable agents in other cities.

5) After questions 1, 2, 3, & 4 have been answered, do I stay in the home or move?

The real estate agent can help you determine the financial and emotional consequences of both scenarios.

Should you decide to move, you need to commit to the real estate agent to be your seller's agent in selling your home and to be your buyer's agent in the purchase of your new residence assuming you are going to stay in Kansas City.

At your initial meeting, the real estate agent should clarify the alternative agency relationships available both in Kansas and Missouri. The agent at that time should also explain the meaning of the terms *buyer's agent* and *seller's agent,* as well as *designated* and *dual agent* and *transactional broker.*

Life does indeed become complicated. Divorce adds significantly to this complication, and assistance must be sought in many areas. Since one's home is typically a person's major financial investment, professional real estate advice is a necessity in a divorce situation. The repercussions of uninformed real estate decisions can be very serious and costly. A divorced person must seek the best professional real estate advice available. Finding the best and most experienced agent is crucial.

LEGAL TIP:
If you move to a new state, your prior decree is enforceable under the full faith and credit provisions of the U.S. Constitution.

SURVIVING DIVORCE

Resource Listing

CREDIT/DEBT COUNSELING

Action Credit Advisors
816/472-1234

All American Credit Clearing
816/765-2600

Consumer Credit Counseling Service
816/753-0535

Kansas City Credit Service
816/421-8001

National Credit Counseling Services
800/844-6227

FINANCIAL ADVISORS REFERRAL

Institute of Certified Financial Planners
800/282-PLAN

FINANCIAL ADVISORS SPECIALIZING IN DIVORCE

Sharon Anne Lockhart
Investment, Management & Research
Prairie Village, KS
913/649-5300

Sandi Weaver
Financial Security Advisors
Kansas City, MO
816/363-0011

Annette Wells
Financial Services
North Kansas City, MO
816/474-9090

MORTGAGE CONSULTANTS

Paula Walter
Associated Capitol
Overland Park, KS
913/338-5550

Chuck Ziegler
Overland Park, KS
913/341-3800

MOVERS

The Real Apartment Movers
816/831-7777

The Real APARTMENT MOVERS® — SINCE 1978

All Prices Contractually Guaranteed in Advance
Call For Details.

APARTMENTS • HOMES • OFFICES • CONDOS

Apartment Movers can move you at prices competitive with truck rental firms.

Moves from $49
EXACT PRICE BY PHONE IN MINUTES – CALL NOW

831-7777

WE MOVE IT LIKE YOU'D MOVE IT – CAREFULLY

DIVORCE $ENSE

Pre-Divorce Financial Planning For Equitable Asset Division

SHARON ANNE LOCKHART, CFP, CDP

A MEMBER OF

ICDP
The Institute for Certified Divorce Planners

INVESTMENT MANAGEMENT & RESEARCH, INC.
Member NASD/SIPC
4200 SOMERSET SUITE 155 PRAIRIE VILLAGE, KS 66208
TEL 913 649 5300   WATS 888 649 5300   FAX 913 649 5302

FINANCIAL – RESOURCE LISTING

ORGANIZATIONS

National Foundation for Consumer Credit
301/589-5600 or 800/388-2227
Spanish 800/682-9832

National Resource Network
214/528-9080

Older Women's League
202/783-6686

Pension Rights Center
202/296-3776

REAL ESTATE SERVICES

The Buyer's Agent
913/338-3880

For Sale By Owner Services
913/498-3726

The Home Network
Overland Park, KS 913/451-3434
Independence, MO 816/478-8800
Raymore, MO 816/322-6300

Claudette Moyer
JC Nichols Real Estate
Prairie Village, KS
913/341-6660

Jeanette K. Lee
REMAX First, REALTORS
Shawnee Mission, KS
913/338-1880

Plaza Living
Kansas City, MO
816/931-3700

Quality Hill Partnership
Kansas City, MO
816/472-1442

RECOMMENDED READING

A Marital Property Handbook – *June Weisberger and Teresa Meuer*

Divorce and Money – *Violet Woodhouse and Victoria Felton-Collins*

Divorce: Playing the Game to Win – *Jan E. Ross and Dianna J. Kremis*

The Dollars and Sense Guide to Divorce: The Financial Guide for Women – *Judith Briles*

The Economics of Divorce: A Financial Survival Kit for Women – *Libbie Agran*

How to Do Better at Collecting Child Support and Alimony – *Robert S. Sigman*

How to Modify and Collect Child Support – *Joseph Matthews*

The Pension Answer Book – *Stephen J. Krass*

Smart Ways to Save Money During and After Divorce – *Victoria E. Collins and Ginita Wall*

Women and Money: The Independent Woman's Guide to Financial Security – *Frances Leonard*

How To Survive DIVORCE

EDUCATIONAL SEMINAR

Learn about:
- Preparing for the Legal Decisions Ahead
- Dividing Property and Assets – What's Best for Me?
- *Plus more from area professionals…*

Every January, May and September • 9-noon
Overland Park, KS • I-435 & Metcalf

Call for information:
Sandi Weaver, CPA, CFP, *Financial Analyst* 363-0011
Chuck Ziegler, *Mortgage Consultant* 341-3800
Connie Russell, LCSW, *Counselor/Career Advisor* 444-5511
Woody Longan, JD, *Attorney* 491-4050

Recovery and Planning for a New Life

Connecting with Self Before Reconnecting 68

Divorce and Vocational Concerns 71

Taking Advantage of the Educational
Opportunities in Kansas City 74

Health and Beauty: Now's the Time to Indulge 75

Your Time Has Come to See the World:
Traveling to and From Kansas City 77

Saving Valuable Time:
Housing/Lawn/Pet Care Services 78

Resource Listing 79

Contributing Writers

ELIZABETH CAMPBELL, PH.D., is a licensed psychologist and a marriage, family and vocational counselor in the Kansas City area. Liz has been helping people with divorce-related issues for many years and delights in helping people find their way through the "work aspects" of divorce.

LOIS A. MILLER, LSCSW, LCSW, is a psychotherapist in private practice. She has been a social worker for 26 years and in private practice for seven years. She has spent many years working in the areas of child abuse and neglect, and adoption. She currently does individual counseling related to depression and anxiety disorders and specializes in marriage, divorce and stepfamily counseling.

CHRISTA NEUNKIRCHEN received her training and certification as an aesthetician in Germany. In 1980, her husband was transferred to the Kansas City area where Christa worked in two different salons before opening up her own salon, European Secret. Christa's staff includes a massage therapist and a cosmetologist technician. European Secret offers many services including facials, pedicures, manicures, waxing and massages. Christa has been in this business for almost 20 years.

SURVIVING DIVORCE

Connecting with Self Before Reconnecting

by Lois A. Miller, LSCSW, LCSW

There is much work to be done on self during the separation, divorce and post-divorce process. This is most important if we hope to have a healthy relationship in the future. But how do we develop self-awareness in order to form a healthy relationship?

The Grieving Process

There are five stages in the grieving process: Denial, bargaining, depression, anger and acceptance. Because these are addressed as stages it is important to realize that this is a "process" and none of the stages comes in neat packages. Many of them overlap and many people feel that their anger or depression has passed only to find that it returns. Grieving can be a very frustrating process but a very necessary one. People often ask, "How long will it take before I feel better?" The timeframe for grieving differs as much as we are all different. I suggest to my clients that they take a year off before forming a new relationship in order to get through the process and to get to know themselves again. I am not suggesting that they don't date or have fun but to avoid forming a serious relationship.

Too many people rebound to another relationship too quickly. They may do this for many reasons. They may not feel "complete" without another person. Rebounding helps us to avoid the grieving process as we get so caught up in the new relationship. Those who have an affair while still in their marriage are rebounding even before they leave the marriage. Rebounding is not healthy and usually leads to an unhealthy relationship.

A thought about depression: All of us experience some form of depression in the grieving process. However, some may experience a more serious form of clinical depression. If you have thoughts of suicide, have trouble sleeping or sleep too much, if your eating patterns have changed significantly, if you have low energy, low concentration, feelings of worthlessness or hopelessness, then it is important that you seek a doctor's advice. Your doctor may prescribe medication to help you with your symptoms. If you suffer from clinical depression you cannot wish it away and it is not a character defect. It simply requires medical attention.

How do we know that we have sufficiently grieved our loss? We know if our feelings are not as intense as they once were. In other words, we are not as angry or sad or upset. We don't totally blame our former spouse but rather can recognize the part we played in the breakup of the marriage. We can recognize that our former spouse has both good qualities and faults, after all, we married them! We can forgive ourselves and our former spouse. That means that we can forgive the person, not condone abusive behavior.

The Beginning Experience weekend is available in the Kansas City area. This is a weekend designed to aid us with the grieving process. It is an excellent tool and I highly recommend it to everyone who experiences loss through death or divorce. Give yourself a gift of this weekend (see page 81).

Family-of-Origin Issues

No, I am not going to "blame" our parents for the way we are. But it is important to recognize that the way we were raised plays an important part in who we are as adults. There are "reasons" we may act as we do, just as our parents had "reasons" for what they did or did not do. There are reasons we chose our marriage partner. We need to discover those reasons so that we make more appropriate choices for our future.

Finian N. Meis, M.A., D.M., and Tara M. Markey-Meis, M.A., developed a marriage preparation program which is nationally used, called "When Families Marry." The concept of two families marrying, not just two people, is important. When we enter a marriage we are bringing everything we learned about finances, communication, sexuality, spirituality, etc., from our family of origin. It is therefore important to be aware of what we learned and also what we didn't learn. It is important to discover what we want to repeat from our family of origin and what we want to discard. These are but a few of the questions that you can ask yourself:

- **Finances:**

  Were they handled responsibly?

  Who paid the bills?

  Who worked outside the home?

  Was mother required to be home with the children?

- **Communication/Anger/Conflict:**

  Did one parent control the other?

  Did one parent do all of the talking?

  Did my parents listen to each other?

  Did my parents fight in front of the children or did they have all disagreements behind closed doors?

  Did my parents fight fair or was there dirty fighting?

  Was there verbal, emotional or physical spousal abuse?

  Did I ever witness my parents resolving conflicts and how did they do that?

  Did one parent always give in, did they take turns, did they compromise, did they agree to disagree or was it always a win-lose dilemma?

- **Sexuality/Intimacy:**

  How were sexuality and intimacy displayed in my family?

  Did my parents openly display affection?

  Was there a warm feeling between my parents or was the air always thick with tension?

  What roles did my parents play?

  Were they traditional male/female roles?

  Was I sexually abused as a child and how does this affect me as an adult?

- **Spirituality:**

  What kind of religious practices did we have?

  Did we pray together as a family? Was spirituality an important aspect in family?

Divorced people have an even more complicated situation. Not only do we need to ask these questions about our family of origin, but we must also ask how these issues were dealt with in our previous marriage(s).

Reasons for the Choice of Our Previous Partner

I view a family as actors in a play. Each person in the family plays a different role. Many believe that birth order contributes to this along with the personality of the person. Different roles can be the caretaker, the sick child, the clown, the troublemaker, the overachiever/hero or the avoidant child. Each of these roles is developed as a coping mechanism to survive as a member of the family. I am not suggesting that all families are abusive or neglectful. What I am saying is that no family is perfect and we all develop roles.

Unfortunately, many families have "family secrets." These secrets include substance abuse, physical abuse, sexual abuse, verbal abuse, emotional abuse and neglect. If this is the case as children we learn that we cannot *trust* the world and our caretakers for stability, consistency and protection from danger. We also feel that we have either been physically or emotionally *abandoned* by those we depend on. "Lack of trust" and "abandonment" are critical issues for persons of divorce.

This creates feelings that we cannot trust another human being. We fear being abandoned and will do anything to save our relationship. Because of our fear of abandonment we become jealous of our partner. We avoid intimacy because we are suspicious and emotionally guarded so as not to be hurt. We have low self-worth and feel that we don't deserve better. We feel that what happened in our family was our fault. Our emotional needs were not met in our family of origin so we attempt to change an emotionally unavailable partner into someone who can meet our needs. We become a caretaker because we were not taken care of, particularly to people who have problems or appear needy. Control becomes a necessity as we had little security as a child.

What we learn in our family of origin are "patterns" of behavior. Even if these patterns are not particularly healthy, that is what we learn and that is usually why we choose the partner whom we marry. We marry what is "known." Even if it is not healthy, it is comfortable.

We don't consciously choose an unhealthy partner. But because we marry "patterns" we may choose an alcoholic, abuser or controller. We may marry for the reason of finally being taken care of, later to realize that it means being controlled. We may marry a passive woman/man because we were dominated by our mother/father. We may marry a domineering, controlling woman/man because our mother/father was controlling. We might marry someone whom we can take care of and change. We may settle for a bad relationship because we don't deserve better. We may marry someone who criticizes us because we could seldom or never measure up to our parents' expectations no matter what we did.

Ways to Avoid Another Unhealthy Relationship

- Grieve previous losses. If you don't, you will be carrying a lot of excess baggage into a new relationship.

- Understand that you are who you are because of how you were raised (once again, no blame, only reasons) along with peer influences and experiences from previous relationships and marriage(s).

- Discover the reasons for the choice of your previous partner.

- Learn the "red flags" of potential partners.

- Pray, read, journal.

- Attend the Beginning Experience weekend.

- Seek counseling to help you through this process.

RECOVERY AND PLANNING

Divorce and Vocational Concerns
by Elizabeth Campbell, Ph.D.

"It never rains, but pours." When it comes to how divorce "rains" on your vocational life that saying was never more true! It pours and pours! Some people find their current jobs threatened, even swept away entirely by the emotional torrents of divorce. Others, in the sudden dropping of the barometer of change, find themselves re-examining everything. Is this what I really want to do? Could I find something different? better?

Under the threatening clouds of financial ruin brought on by divorce, there are those who are pushed to seek a second job or a better paying one. Finding their sheltering roof torn away for the first time in their lives – or the first time since marriage – career homemakers may have to find a way into the employment market. ("What can I do? How can I support myself?")

- Henry has a so-so position as a computer repairman. Ten years ago he went into this field because of the job possibilities. He really didn't care that much for it, but with a family to provide for, he knew he had to hold on. Now his wife and kids are moving to her family back east. The whole picture has changed. Maybe he could find an occupation that turns him on – a true career. Where to start?

- Mavis has made "wife and mother" her whole life. When Bart told her he wanted a divorce so he could marry his legal assistant, she was devastated. Her whole reality flipped. With the children almost grown, she will be alone soon. Without child support and maintenance, finances will become a problem. What does a 40-year-old beginner do? How can she make a life for herself?

- The divorce has flattened Katie. She can't stop crying – even at work. Her job as an office supplies salesperson is sliding downhill. Her boss has given her several warnings about her declining performance. Because she is unable to sleep she can't get up in the morning. Her mind is a jumble. She keeps making mistakes on the few orders she is able to get. She knows she will be fired soon.

- Joan kicked Ansel out of the house six months ago. Because of all the expenses of providing for her and the three boys, he has little left to live on himself. He has been bunking in with a friend, but that can't go on much longer. The only thing he can think of is a second job. But what?

- It takes a lot of money to bring up four children these days. The court ordered Joe to pay Leslie meager child support – not enough to get by on. Since the divorce, Joe has really fallen apart. He drinks too much. He's laid off a lot. He pays child support late, or partially, or both. Often he doesn't pay at all. Leslie can't go on living in this uncertainty. She's got to get a better job, take in washing on the side – or something!

Each of these people is going to have to think hard and heavy, and soon, about work. Henry – about changing his job. Mavis – about entering the world of paid work for the first time. Katie – about holding onto the position she has. Ansel – about increasing his diminishing income. And Leslie – about finding a way to a secure, stable living.

> **LEGAL TIP:**
> All alimony and support payments should be by check or a signed, dated receipt should be obtained. The receiving party should keep a very accurate record of all payments received.

Bottom line: During divorce and for the first year or so, you need to keep stress levels down as much as possible. That means you must limit change where you can. This isn't the time to chuck it all and try beach bumming in Bermuda. If you have a job, keep it for the time being. After things calm down a bit, you can assess your situation: So Henry and Katie need to stick with their current jobs and stay if at all possible.

Second: Look before you leap! When we're under pressure, our whole body signals, "Go, go, go!" We want to take action – any action! Hold it! Before you quilt together a resume, think! Then think again! Ansel and Leslie may rush into a "minimum wager" at McDonald's, thus exhausting themselves and gaining little after deductions.

I'm going to suggest a step-by-step approach:

- FIRST: Clarify your thoughts
- SECOND: Assess your –
  - Options
  - Yourself
  - Work World
  - Job Market
- THIRD: Decide – Job, training, or both?
- FOURTH: Plan
- FIFTH: Seek Support

First of all, you aren't likely in a position to think clearly at this time. Feelings are overwhelming. Now *is* the time to journal. Now *is* the time to talk to others – family, friends, your minister, your divorce support group. Eventually you may feel strong enough to seek professional help: a vocational, mental health, or marriage and family counselor.

You may want to get the services of a financial advisor as well. After all, it's important to know what your money situation is as well as where you, personally, are coming from. (Ask your banker, attorney, accountant, counselor, minister, or former school counselor for a recommendation or see page 64.)

This isn't the time to pull the covers over your head and hibernate.

Next you need to take an inventory. "Who am I?" "What can I do?" "What are my interests?" "Where would I like to work?" "Do I want to work for myself?" "Where can I get the training I need?" "Do I need to go back to school?" These are serious questions – and often they go unanswered as we go through life browsing on the chances that come our way. Have you ever thought that work could be your joy? Have you ever dreamed that you could earn more doing what you want to do?

How will you do this? Besides the counselors I've already told you about, there are other options.

- The Missouri and Kansas Division of Employment Security has testing, job counseling, and placement services that are absolutely free.
- Your local community, four-year college, or university has a career service that is low- to no-cost.

RECOVERY AND PLANNING

- Make an appointment with your old high school counseling center for information about evaluation services.
- The Community Mental Health Centers, Catholic Services, and Jewish Vocational Services offer some assistance in this arena. Some large churches have limited help.

That isn't enough, though. You have to investigate what's out there. You've figured out that you need at least fifty thousand for a four-hour day, three-day week in which you are your own boss working with the rich and famous in Capri. It would be a good idea to check out whether the position exists, or could! Most of the services that help you figure out who you are and what you want also have resources for exploring careers. Some have computer search facilities. Others have libraries of job information. Don't overlook your local research librarian – college or public. Spend an afternoon going through the bookstore. What they have is "hot" and readable.

Only now do you get to the job market itself. At this point you can look through the want ads. But not till now. You are perusing them to analyze availabilities – not to get a job. A good counselor will help you further identify what the trends and opportunities are.

You are ready for a preliminary decision. "Will I go for a new job, rehab the one I have, or keep my status quo while I retool?" The decision tree at this point takes you to a resume, a further search for training, or an "action plan" for making what you now have more serviceable.

This is a complicated process. Don't even think about going it alone. Ask for help – professional and personal.

Caution: Many professional head hunters are looking to fill jobs rather than to find the best job for *you*. Many commercial placement services charge a big fee up front or a large percentage of your first year's salary. Others will take you through the process for big bucks, but give no guarantee they will get you work. Examine these carefully and use them only after you are fully informed about exactly what they will do for you and how much your commitment will be.

LEGAL TIP:

You may have liability for some charges made on joint credit cards, so all credit cards with your name on them should be retrieved if possible.

Taking Advantage of the Educational Opportunities in Kansas City

by Linda Sanchez

Many individuals experiencing a divorce are forced to go back to school, receive training and create and/or improve their current job situation in order to maintain their lifestyle. Ultimately, many individuals find that additional education and training not only maintains but can improve their lifestyle. It can also improve their outlook on life in general. An added bonus to taking classes is that this is an opportunity for you to meet people, many in the same situation as you.

Kansas City residents are fortunate to have area colleges and universities which offer classes and degree programs in everything from agriculture to zoology. Within a half-hour drive of the metro area there's a wide range of higher education choices including two major universities, several colleges, three medical schools, a law school, a conservatory of music and one of the nation's best art schools. This area also has a community college network that is one of the largest and best-funded in the country.

Whether you are interested in pursuing an undergraduate or graduate degree, receiving business training, improving upon existing job skills, or even learning how to grow perennials, Kansas City has it all. Students can choose from courses at community colleges, private four-year colleges, and state-supported universities including the University of Missouri-Kansas City and branch campuses of Central Missouri State, Kansas State University, the University of Kansas and the University of Missouri-Columbia.

There are also informal training opportunities offered through various sources including Communiversity, the Parks and Recreation Departments and the Kansas City Libraries.

For more information or academic advice, call the admissions office at the colleges or universities in which you are interested. Counselors at area community colleges have information about courses and degree programs of all colleges and universities in the Kansas City area as well as information on receiving financial assistance. The community colleges also provide free career counseling services for residents of Kansas or Missouri.

Check with your local library and bookstores to explore alternative learning opportunities. The following resource section (see page 79) provides a partial list of institutions, organizations and training centers in the area.

RECOVERY AND PLANNING

Health and Beauty: Now's the Time to Indulge
Special relaxation treatments (for women _and_ men)

by Christa Neunkirchen

Change can be bewildering, even paralyzing. But with the right attitude and skills, you can survive change. Learn to embrace change and you may even profit from it. Don't focus on the passing of the "good old days." They won't be back. Instead, be willing to move ahead and make change a positive presence in your life.

Even a small amount of change can make a big difference in your day-to-day life. Unfortunately, it also can have an impact on your appearance. The muscles in your neck and back tighten, your skin can break out in blemishes or a rash, and even your hair can become lackluster or unmanageable when you undergo an unusual amount of stress.

It is now especially important to treat yourself to new or enhanced ways of taking care of your skin and your body. The following are just a few of the more popular treatments both men and women can experience.

Art of Massage

Massage can be defined as the manual manipulation of the soft tissue of the body and is the most natural and instinctive means of relieving pain. Relaxation therapy combines massage with use of moisturizing oils and relaxing music to create a unique, stress-free environment. The human touch has the power to console, relax and heal. The power of touch can:

- Reduce stress
- Relieve back and neck pain
- Increase circulation
- Increase energy
- Moisturize the skin
- Relax and invigorate the body

Facial Massage

There are energy pressure points in the face, neck and shoulders which have been used for centuries to revitalize and rejuvenate the body/mind system. Facial massage incorporates these pressure points and is a gentle and pleasant experience. It can help restore the face to a childlike freshness while imparting a sense of spiritual uplifting. Massaging the face, neck and shoulders is a totally invigorating experience that also provides an introduction of another form of body work. It is a wonderful experience.

Something magical happens as your whole body lets go and its energy is shifted into a more peaceful place.

Pedicure and Foot Massage

When your feet hurt, your entire body hurts along with them. During a pedicure, your feet are soaked in a hot herbal foot bath. A hot foot soak helps improve circulation and softens the tissue making the foot more receptive to a massage. The massage also helps relieve acute pains due to stress tensions. Walking can once again become a pleasure.

Other services to look for can include:

- Herbal Deep and Lactose Enzyme Peels (face)
- 10 Minute Stress Relieving Massage (neck and shoulders)
- Deep Conditioning Hair Treatment
- Aromatherapy Scalp Treatment
- Manicure (hands and nails)
- Paraffin Bath (warm wax treatment for the hands and feet)

What to Look for in a Salon

There are various salons in the Kansas City area that offer these and other treatments. However, when selecting your salon be sure to look for cleanliness in both the staff and facility. Also be sure to select a salon and staff that have the proper state licensure. Professional memberships and special recognitions also can be a sign of a creditable salon or day spa. Most importantly, don't be afraid to ask about the background and training of the individual who will be providing these services. Trust is a vital component in the art of relaxation

Prices

Prices of these and other treatments can vary throughout the country. However an approximate price range for the Kansas City area:

Manicure	$15 - $25
Facial	$30 - $75
Pedicure	$25 - $35
Massage	$10 - $60

Some salons offer a package price or day spa packages which can include 4-6 treatments and a lunch or snack. These packages can range from $100-$200.

It can also be helpful to indulge in some of these treatments in order to learn how to treat yourself at home. Learning to provide yourself with a manicure or pedicure using supplies from your local drugstore is an economical way to take care of yourself. However, nothing takes the place of escaping to a salon and having someone pamper you for even one hour.

With these treatments, you can learn to enjoy doing something for yourself. Take a stress time-out. It's important to keep in mind that some stress is normal. In fact it's a way of life. However, when things begin to get too serious, take a break and remove yourself from the stressful situation. Treat yourself to a facial, massage, or pedicure. You can feel more relaxed after your treatment and ready to face additional challenges with a more positive outlook.

RECOVERY AND PLANNING

Your Time Has Come to See the World: Traveling to and From Kansas City

by Linda Sanchez

Taking time for yourself during a divorce is very important for your mental health and well-being. Whether you decide to go away for a weekend to enjoy solitude and self-reflection or start a new vacation tradition as a single parent, Kansas City offers wonderful opportunities for all kinds of travel within all kinds of budgets.

Kansas City is the most centrally located principal city in the United States. Its unique location makes it a natural transportation center with quick and easy access to the rest of the country. Three interstate highways intersect at Kansas City, I-70, I-35 and I-29. Greater Kansas City is also the nation's second largest rail center with twelve rail lines that include four passenger lines daily to many U.S. cities. Every major U.S. passenger airline serves the Kansas City area with airfares for origination and destination among the lowest in the nation.

Since it is now established that you live in one of the most accessible cities in the nation, taking a few days for exploring and self-discovery may be a good idea. If you choose to take your children along, there is no better opportunity to have fun together, to rest, explore new places, and most important, gather some perspectives on the new life you are now building together.

Before you go, collect as much information as you possibly can about your destination. Get pamphlets, brochures, magazines, articles and library books. Call the state tourist office and town chambers of commerce for more specific information.

Try to schedule a balance of activity and rest each day. Remember, planning your day is important, so sit down and make a list of everything you hope to do or see. Then, eliminate half the list by concentrating on everyone's "can't miss" list. Be flexible and be ready to make contingency plans depending on the weather or other unpredictable circumstances, especially if you bring children.

If you choose to go on vacation by yourself or with friends, there are also many "non-traditional" vacations available. These can include adventure vacations based on individual hobbies or sports such as canoeing, hiking, rafting, cycling, camping, sailing or riding horses. For a longer vacation, there are also many overseas destinations which can be surprisingly affordable and very enjoyable.

For information on these vacations as well as information on how to plan, where to stay, low-cost destinations, etc., go to your local library or bookstore. There are hundreds of books which can provide this information along with resource addresses and telephone numbers. Also, use the Internet if it is available to you. The web offers information and even photos of hotels, along with prices and 800 # hotlines to call for more information about national and international destinations.

The following resource section (see page 82) will provide you with telephone numbers of Kansas City resources to help you plan your trip. Bon Voyage!

SURVIVING DIVORCE

Saving Valuable Time: Housing/Lawn/Pet Care Services

by Linda Sanchez

If you felt that there was a shortage of time prior to your divorce, you probably have less of it now. Between your job, legal negotiations, packing, transporting children, and managing the household chores, making time for yourself can seem quite hopeless. Yet, as mentioned in previous chapters of this publication, taking time for yourself is critical in the recovery process.

If you've dismissed the idea of getting help with the household tasks before, now would be the time to consider it. Kansas City has many services available, including house cleaning, lawn maintenance, pet walking and even pet waste removal. These services vary in price. However, most businesses will work with you to evaluate your needs and provide something within your budget.

For instance, it would be great to have someone come to your house every day to vacuum, dust and do the laundry. However, the reality is that most cleaning needs can be met with a weekly, biweekly or even a monthly visit by a cleaning service. It may also be that you enjoy doing some of these household chores (yard work or walking the dog), and perhaps hiring someone to fill in the work gaps left by the spouse would suffice.

If hiring someone to help with the household chores is not an option, consider prioritizing and letting certain tasks go undone. Ask a friend or your counselor to help you compose a list of priorities. They can provide a new perspective on these tasks or possibly offer different ideas on how to accomplish them. You also may be surprised by the number of friends or neighbors who want to help you but don't know how. Talking with them about these new challenges can provide this opportunity to them.

Whatever the case, treating yourself to a service not considered under normal circumstances can be a great treat for you and your family. If having more time for yourself isn't enough of a reason, perhaps having more time to spend with your children is – especially now. The following section provides a list of some of the Kansas City services available.

Resource Listing

EDUCATION/EMPLOYMENT TRAINING

Adult Education
Bonner Springs, KS
913/441-6325

Adult Education and GED Testing
*High School and
College Credit available*
Paola, KS
913/294-3379

El Centro – Family Improvement
Kansas City, KS
913/677-1115

Full Employment Council
Main Office: 816/471-2330
Adult Basic Education: 816/474-6401
Employment Service Centers:
- 816/471-1430
- 816/468-8767
- 816/254-3297
Training Center: 816/471-5872

Greater Kansas City Council on Philanthropy
Job Hotline: 816/931-6913

Heartland Works
Kansas City, KS 913/342-9675
Shawnee Mission, KS 913/236-6500

Jobcore
Kansas City, KS 913/281-1710
Kansas City, MO 816/921-3366

Job Service
Kansas City, MO
816/453-4900

Johnson County Community College
Overland Park, KS
913/469-3870
913/469-3836

Kansas City Kansas Adult Education
Kansas City, KS
913/342-5008

Has Life Thrown You a Curve?

Turn to Johnson County Community College for assistance when faced with life-changing decisions. Our educational assistance and planning programs include:

- The **"Choices"** program through the Career Center – helping you make educational decisions that support your career and life goals. The staff can help you get back on the right track.

To learn more about the "Choices" program, call 469-3870.

- **Adult enrichment courses** through the Community Services Division – providing you with numerous courses that are economically priced with flexible class times. It's a perfect opportunity to meet other people with whom you share common interests.

For a list of adult enrichment courses, call 469-3836.

JCCC … It's Where You Belong

Johnson County Community College • 12345 College Blvd. • Overland Park, KS 66210

SURVIVING DIVORCE

Kansas City Kansas Community College
Kansas City, KS
913/321-5949
913/371-2904
913/334-1100

Midwest Career Development Service
Kansas City, KS
913/621-6348

Officemates 5 / Day Star
Overland Park, KS
913/661-9111

HEALTH AND WELLNESS

Tom Jacobs
Yoga Classes
816/619-3499

Christa Neunkirchen
European Secret Face & Body Care
Prairie Village, KS
913/648-3161

Rebecca Paden
Restoration Therapy – Therapeutic and Wellness Massage
Overland Park, KS
913/469-0500

Suzette Scholtes
The Yoga Studio of Johnson County
Merriam, KS
913/492-9598

HOME DECORATING

Connie Pryde Perucca
Specializing in interior mural and sponge painting
Kansas City, MO
816/931-2050

Willhite's Painting
Interior/Exterior Painting
Overland Park, KS
913/642-5708

HOUSE CLEANING

AAA House & Window Cleaning
Shawnee Mission, KS
913/262-3951

Lulu & Mimi Housecleaners
Shawnee Mission, KS
913/649-6022

OfficeMates5 / DayStar
America's Office Staffing Specialists

We specialize in Permanent Staffing for Kansas City

Free computer training for skill enhancement
* **Never a fee to you**

* Customer Service   * Administrative Assts.
* Inside Sales   * Accounting - A/R, A/P
* General Office   * Many other possibilities

Founded in 1957, we are committed to helping you secure the career opportunity for you and your skill set. Please give us a call to see what we have to offer.

(913) 661-9111

9401 Indian Creek Pkwy, Suite 920
Overland Park, KS 66210

RECOVERY AND PLANNING – RESOURCE LISTING

JEWELRY DESIGN

Vinca
Kansas City, MO
816/531-5591

LAWN MAINTENANCE

Hunt's Lawn Service
Louisburg, KS
913/649-7312

VanBooven Lawn & Landscaping
Merriam, KS
913/722-3275

PET SERVICES

Lett's Petts
Overland Park, KS
913/649-5020

Nall Hills Grooming
Overland Park, KS
913/383-2922

Happy Tails Pet Service
Shawnee Mission, KS
913/492-4746

RECOMMENDED READING

The Complete Divorce Recovery Handbook: Grief, Stress, Guilt, Children, Co-Dependence, Self-Esteem, Dating, Remarriage – *John P. Splinter*

Coping with Marital Transitions: A Family Systems Perspective – *Mavis Hetherington*

Divorce and New Beginnings: An Authoritative Guide to Recovery and Growth, Solo Parenting, and Stepfamilies – *Genevieve Clapp*

Divorced Families: Meeting the Challenge of Divorce and Remarriage – *Constance R. Aborns* and *Roy H. Rodgers*

Divorce Hangover: A Step-by-Step Prescription for Creating a Bright Future After Your Marriage Ends – *Anne Walther*

The Ex-Wife Syndrome: Cutting the Cord and Breaking Free After the Marriage Is Over – *Sandra S. Kahn*

Successful Single Parenting – *Gary Richmond*

SINGLES SUPPORT/ACTIVITIES

The Beginning Experience
A non-profit international peer-ministry organization which provides many services to help the widowed, separated and divorced.
913/262-9037

Midwest Singles Dance
Dances held in both
Kansas and Missouri
Dance Hotline: 816/254-6493

The Village Church Singles Ministry
913/262-4200

Singles Program Information Line
913/262-3195

What's Going on in KC?
Look On-line:
http://www.kansascity.com

Midwest Singles Dance
FREE MEMBERSHIP
Live Bands • Large Crowds

Dances held on Friday and Sunday evenings at the finest hotels in Kansas and Missouri. Great way to make new friends.

Dance Hotline Updated Weekly
Call 254-6493.

Emmanuel Baptist Church
Single Adults

10100 Metcalf Ave., Overland Park, KS 66212
Phone 649-0900   Fax 649-0984   www.ebconthehill.org

Paul Geldart
Minister with Single Adults

SURVIVING DIVORCE

TRAVEL INFORMATION

Area libraries offer books on daytrips to international travel from Kansas City – also check with area bookstores.

Johnson County Public Library
913/495-2400

Kansas City Public Library
816/221-2685

Kansas City Kansas Public Library
913/596-5800

Mid-Continent Public Library
816/836-5200

North Kansas City Public Library
816/221-3360

Olathe Public Library
913/764-2259

TRAVEL SERVICES

American Airlines
800-433-7300

AmTrak National Rail Passenger Service
Passenger Information and Tickets
816/421-3622

Continental Airlines
816/471-3700

Delta Airlines
800-221-1212

Northwest Airlines
800-225-2525

Southwest Airlines
800-435-9792

TWA
800-221-2000

United Airlines
800-241-6522

VOCATIONAL COUNSELING

Boas Associates, L.C.
Kansas City, MO
816/363-1500

Elizabeth Campbell
Campbell and Associates
Kansas City, MO
816/361-2030

James C. Heryer
College Guidance & Placement
816/531-2706

New Perspectives
Career Transition Program
816/858-3723

Connie Russell
Centerpoint Counseling and Recovery
Kansas City, MO
816/444-5511

NEW PERSPECTIVES
(816) 858-3723

A Career Transition Program for Single Parents and Displaced Homemakers

The following services are available to you free of charge:
* Career Counseling
* Vocational Aptitude and Interest Testing
* Financial Aid Assistance
* Education and Technical Training Referral

We Help People Help Themselves!

 Boas Associates, L.C.

- Career Management Center
- Business Management Advisors
- Human Resource Consultants

8301 State Line Road, Suite 202 • Kansas City, MO 64114
816.363.1500 • FAX 816.363.2944 • cmc@kcnet.com

Index of Resource Listings

– A –

American Academy of
Matrimonial Lawyers
.... Inside Front Cover, 37, 52

Arbitration/Mediation Services .. 53

Area Bar Associations 53

– C –

Child Care Information 32

Child Support Information 32

Counseling 32-34

Counseling and
Mediation Services 33-34

Credit/Debt Counseling 64

– E –

Education/Employment
Training 79-80, 82

– F –

Financial Advisors
Specializing in Divorce 64

Financial Advisors Referral 64

– H –

Health and Wellness 80

Home Decorating 80

House Cleaning 80

– J –

Jewelry Design 3, 81

– L –

Lawn Maintenance 81

Legal Services
.... Inside Front Cover, 53, 54-56

– M –

Miscellaneous Information 55

Misc/Referral Services 33

Mortgage Consultants
.... Inside Back Cover, 64

Movers 64

– O –

Organizations 33, 34, 55, 65

– P –

Personal and Professional
Coaching 34-35

Pet Services 81

– R –

Real Estate Services 65

Recommended Reading
.... 34, 56, 65, 81

Recommended Reading
For Parents 35

– S –

Seminar 65

Singles Support/Activities 81

Support Groups/
Workshops 33-36

– T –

Travel Information 82

Travel Services 82

– V –

Vocational Counseling 79-80, 82

83

SURVIVING DIVORCE

Notes

Notes

IN KANSAS CITY

Second Edition Now Available to Kansas City Residents!

Getting married, having children, moving to a new town... all of these are major transitions in life and chances are you can easily get your hands on numerous books that will take you step-by-step throughout each phase. Why is divorce not addressed in the same way? Divorce is a transition which has been truly neglected by the directory publishing industry – until now.

Surviving Divorce in Kansas City is the only publication which can provide you with a complete guide to surviving divorce and includes:

- **Advice and direction** from Kansas City experts on topics ranging from when to seek counseling, how to find the right attorney, financial planning, helping your children survive, changing or beginning a career and more.

- **Information about the opportunities** in Kansas City for education, travel and social activities which can help start you on the road to recovery and self-fulfillment.

- **Resource names and telephone numbers** of area professionals and organizations available to help you navigate successfully through your divorce.

Surviving Divorce in Kansas City is the only local resource available to help you, your friend or family member experiencing divorce in Kansas City survive and plan for a better future.

Order your copy today! Complete the order form below and send to:
Surviving Divorce in Kansas City, P.O. Box 1271, Mission, Kansas 66222-0271.
Include $9.95 plus $3.00 postage and handling.

For information regarding a bulk order discount please call (913) 789-7898.

------------------------✂--

Yes! Send me _____ copies of ***Surviving Divorce in Kansas City*** at $9.95 each.
Please add $3.00 postage and handling. Allow 30 days for delivery.

Name _____

Address _____

City _____ State _____ Zip _____

*Please make your checks payable to **Surviving Divorce in Kansas City**.*

Money Back Guarantee
I understand that if I am not satisfied with ***Surviving Divorce in Kansas City,*** I may return the undamaged book within 10 days for a complete refund of the purchase price.